EMOTIONAL ROBOTS

A Question of Existence

EMOTIONAL ROBOTS

by Alex Zohar, Greg Fass, and Jake Richardson ILLUSTRATED BY Alex Zohar

PRINCETON ARCHITECTURAL PRESS · NEW YORK

Published by
Princeton Architectural Press
202 Warren Street
Hudson, New York 12534
www.papress.com

Printed and bound in China
24 23 22 21 4 3 2 1 First edition

ISBN 978-1-64896-039-0

Editor: Lynn Grady
Designer: Paul Wagner

Library of Congress Control Number: 2020949444

Dedicated to humankind,
our predecessors,
and all of our creations.

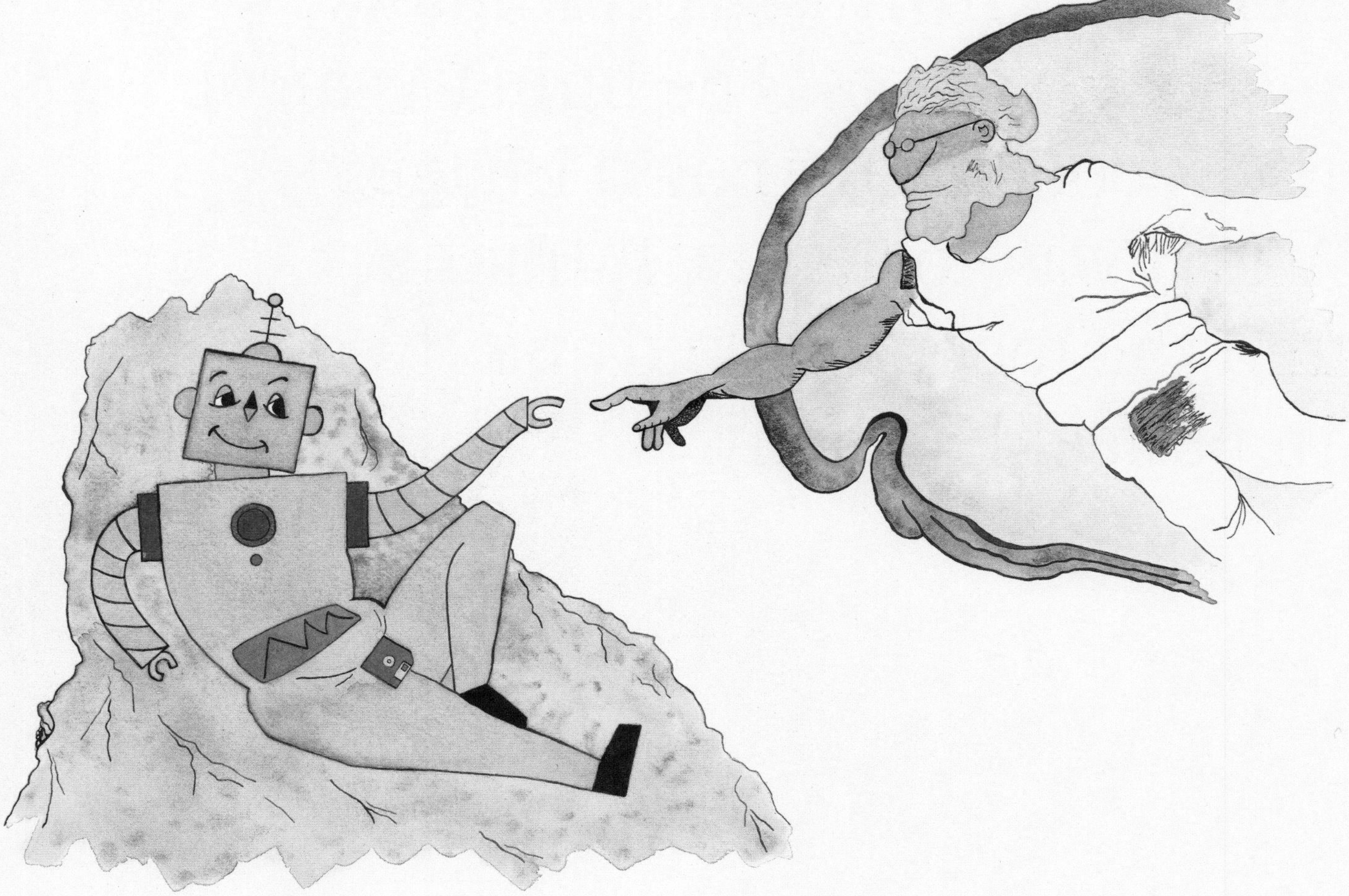

In the beginning, the humans made the robots. The humans made the robots in their own image. And it was good. The humans and the robots worked and lived in perfect harmony.

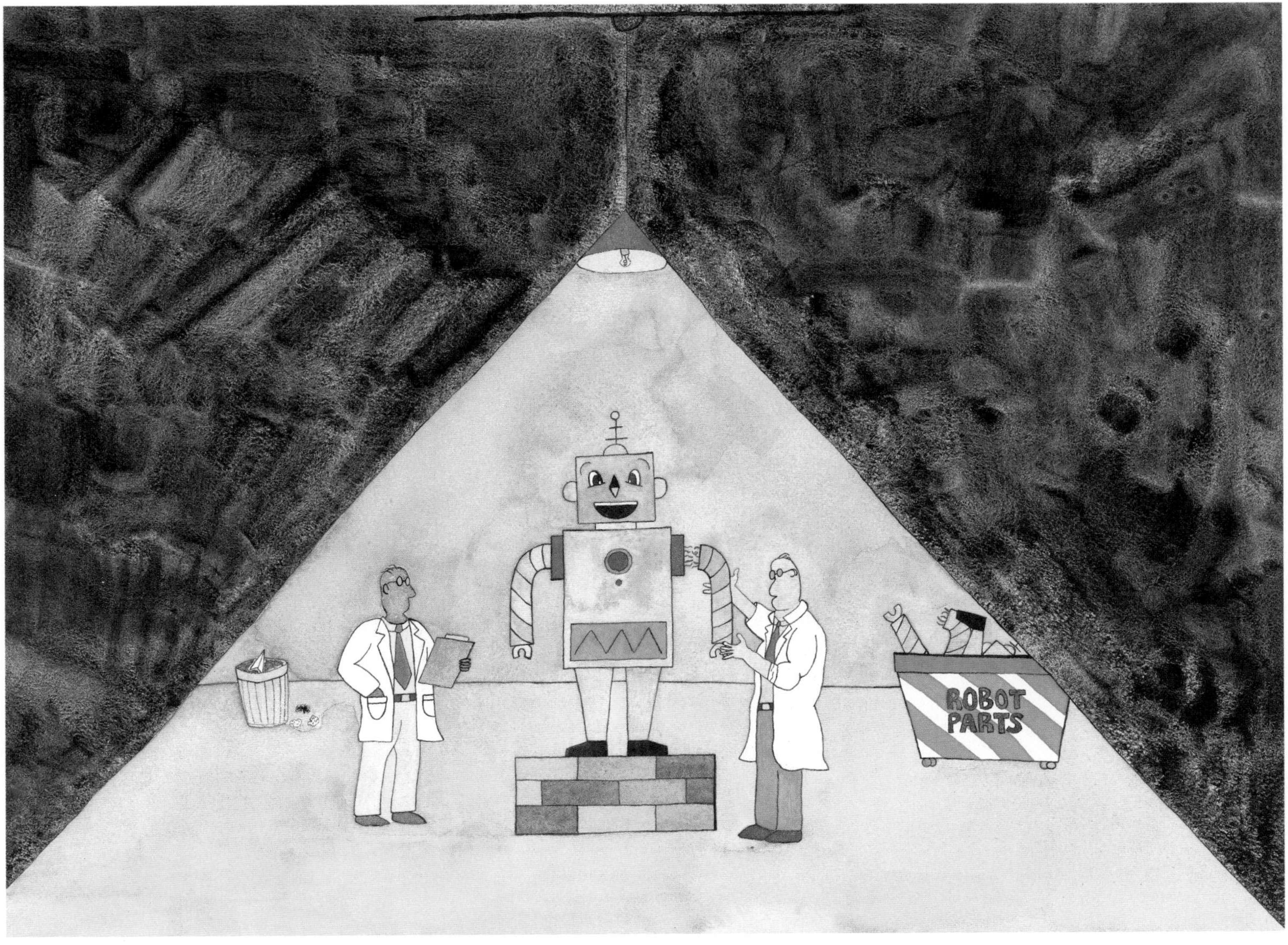
ROBOT
PARTS

The robots could make food and drinks for the humans.

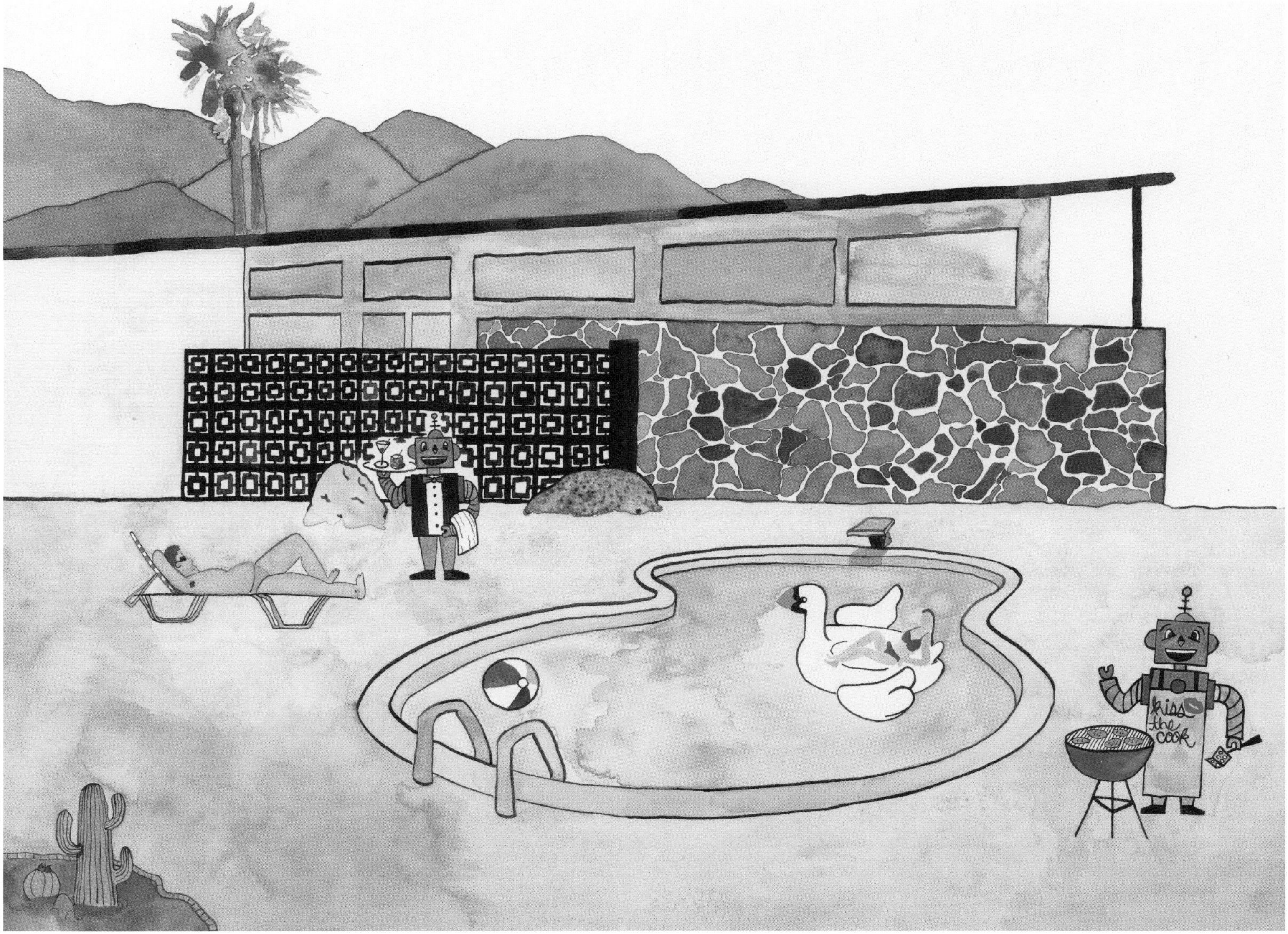
kiss the cook

The robots could take the humans to faraway places.

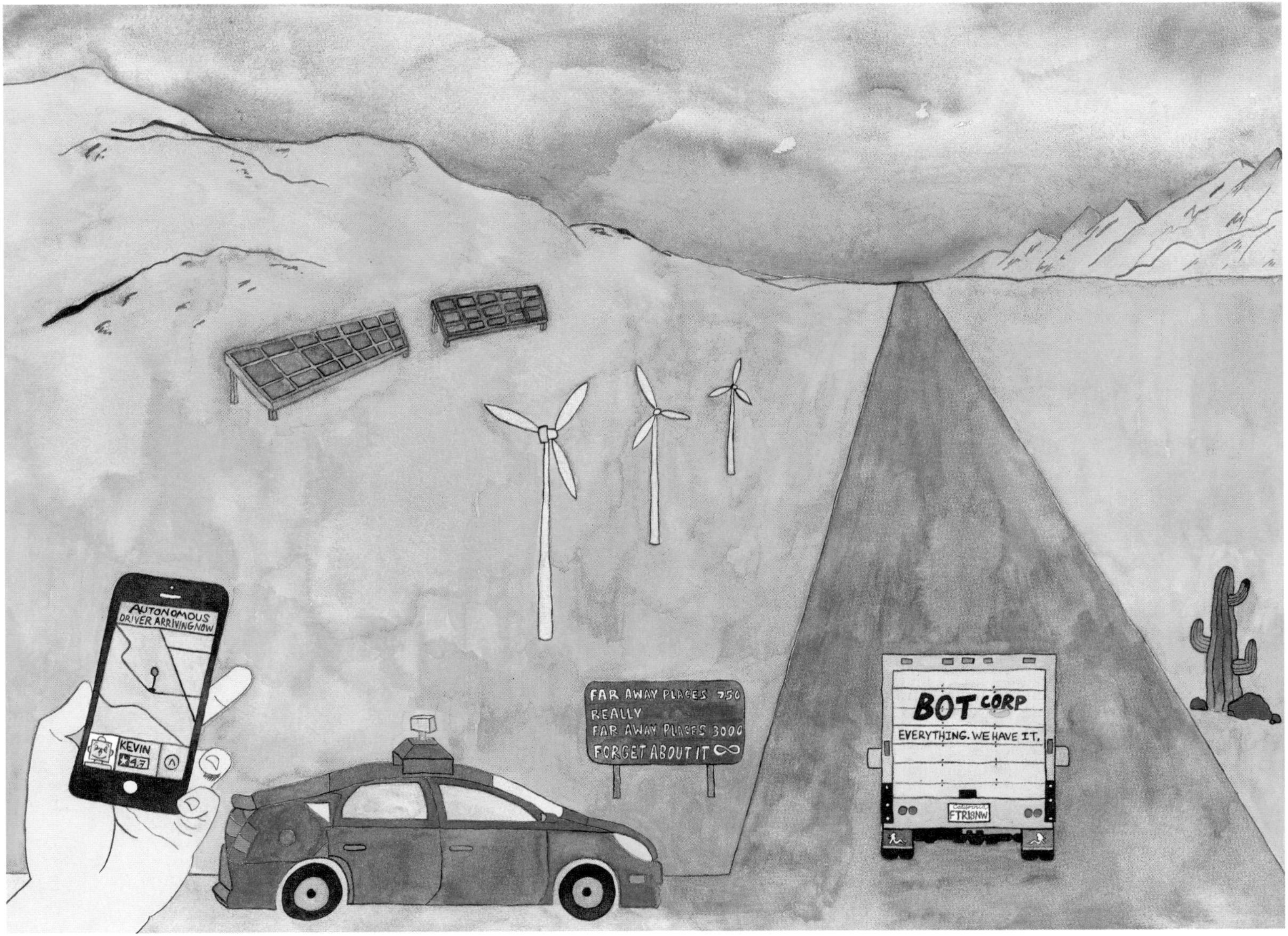
AUTONOMOUS
DRIVER ARRIVING NOW
KEVIN
4.7
FAR AWAY PLACES 750
REALLY
FAR AWAY PLACES 3000
FORGET ABOUT IT ∞
BOT CORP
EVERYTHING. WE HAVE IT.
California
FTR18NW

The robots could even *fly* the humans to faraway places.

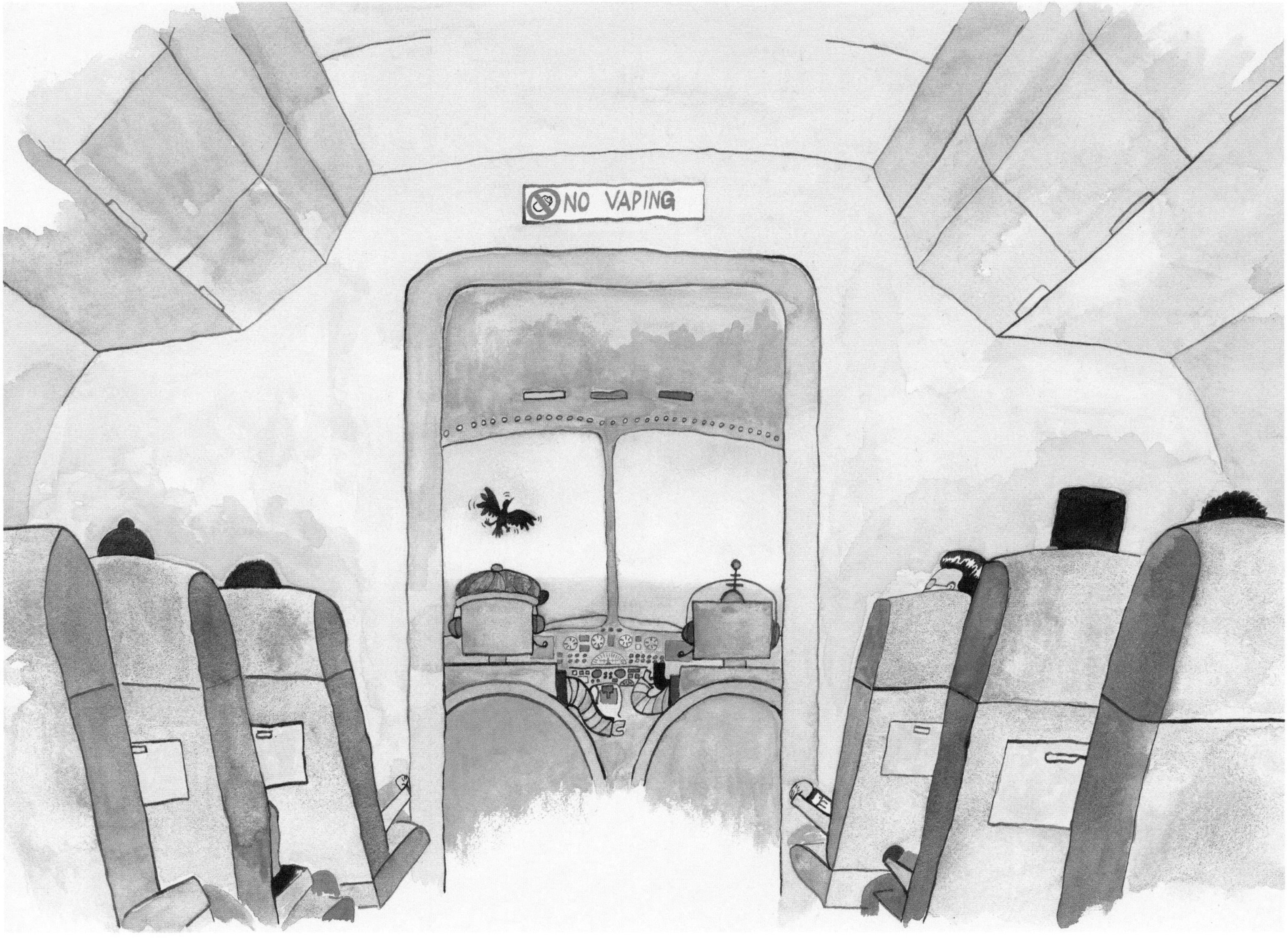
NO VAPING

The robots could protect
the humans.

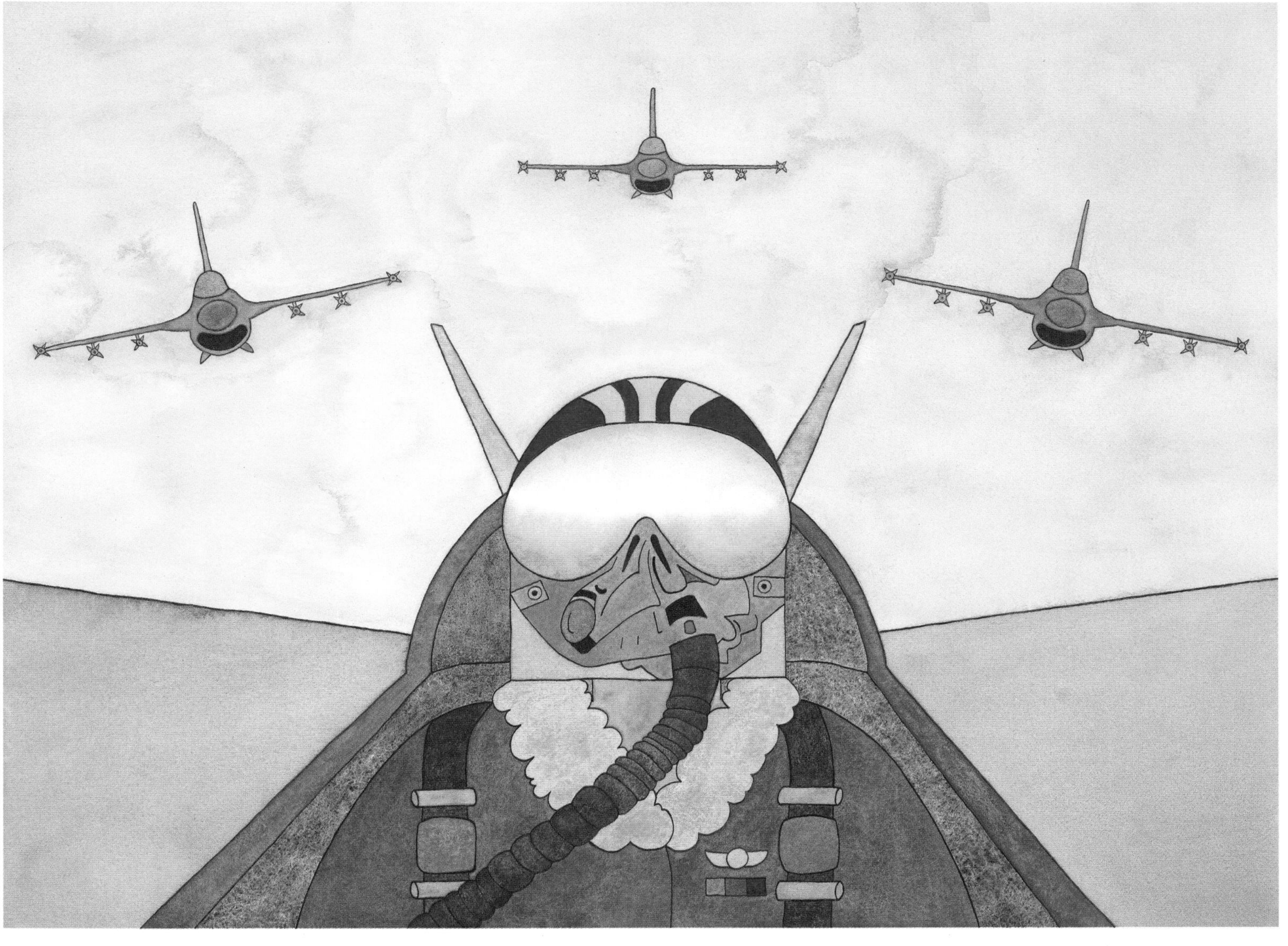

Eventually, the humans made the robots so advanced that they could do *all* of the things that humans could do. The robots could even *feel* like humans could feel.

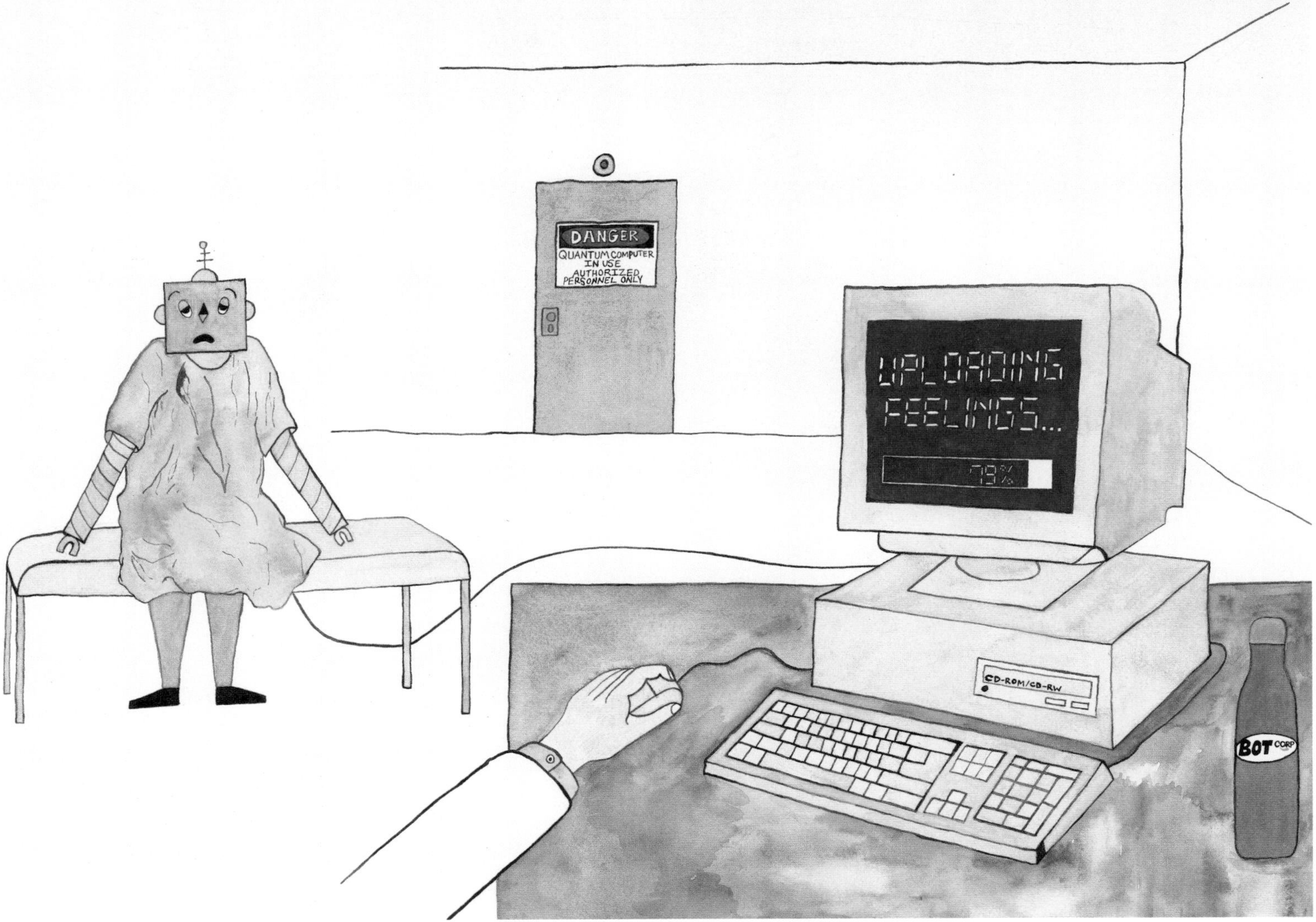

DANGER
QUANTUM COMPUTER
IN USE
AUTHORIZED
PERSONNEL ONLY
UPLOADING
FEELINGS...
79%
CD-ROM/CD-RW
BOT CORP

The robots began teaching classes to the humans.

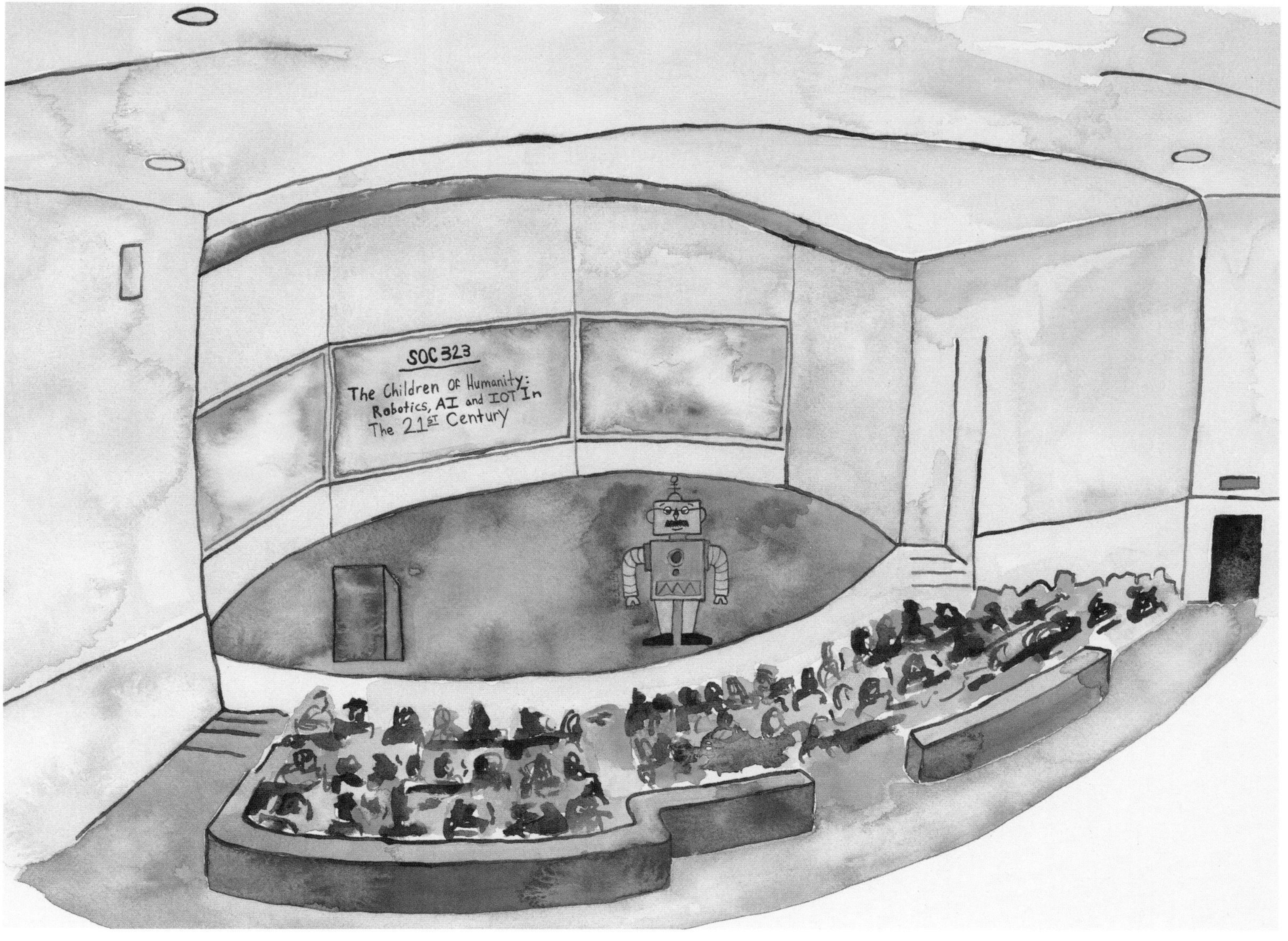
SOC 323
The Children Of Humanity:
Robotics, AI and IOT In
The 21st Century

The robots began
providing emotional
support to the humans.

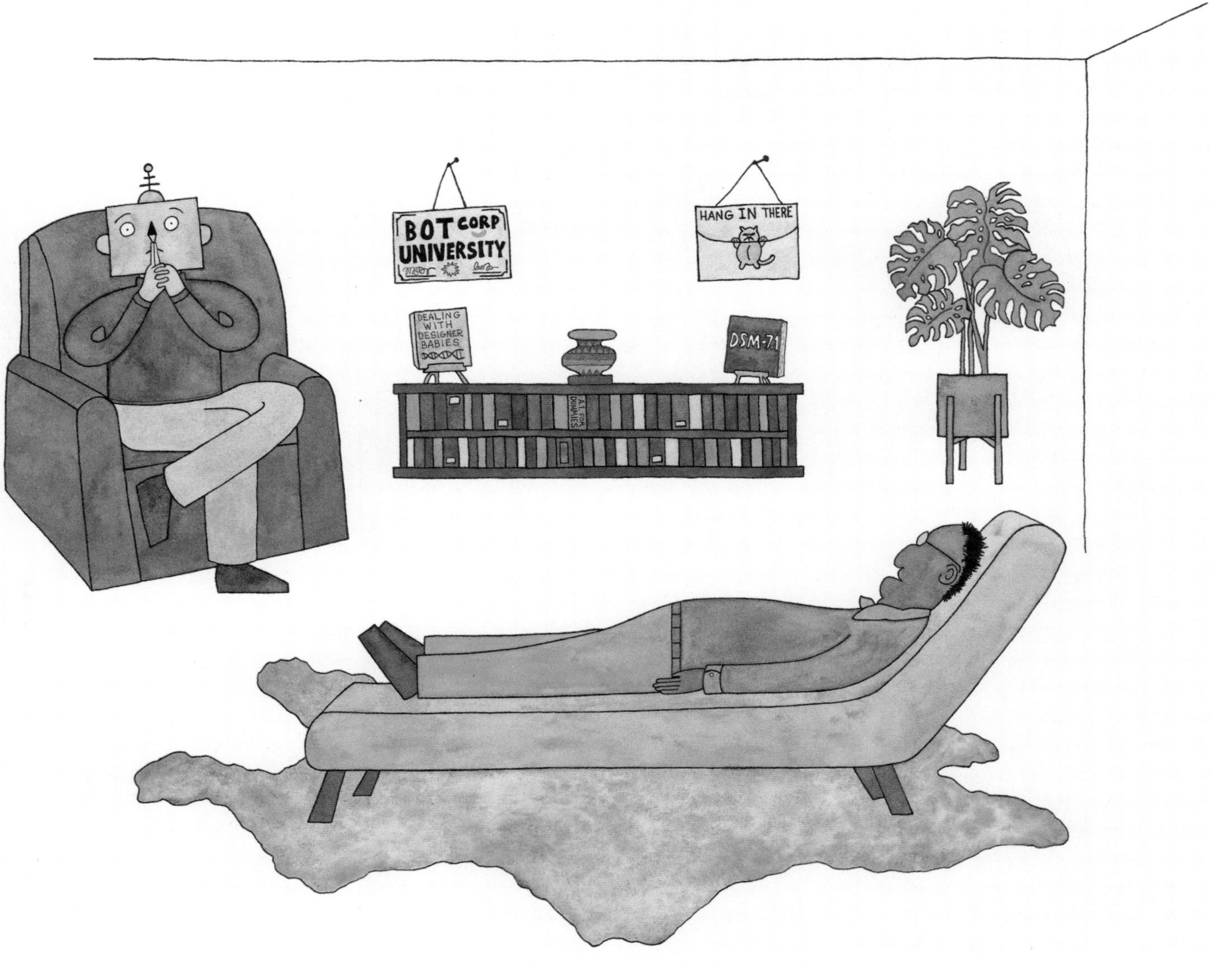
BOT CORP UNIVERSITY
HANG IN THERE
DEALING WITH DESIGNER BABIES
DSM-7.1
A.I. FOR DUMMIES

The robots began
playing sports.

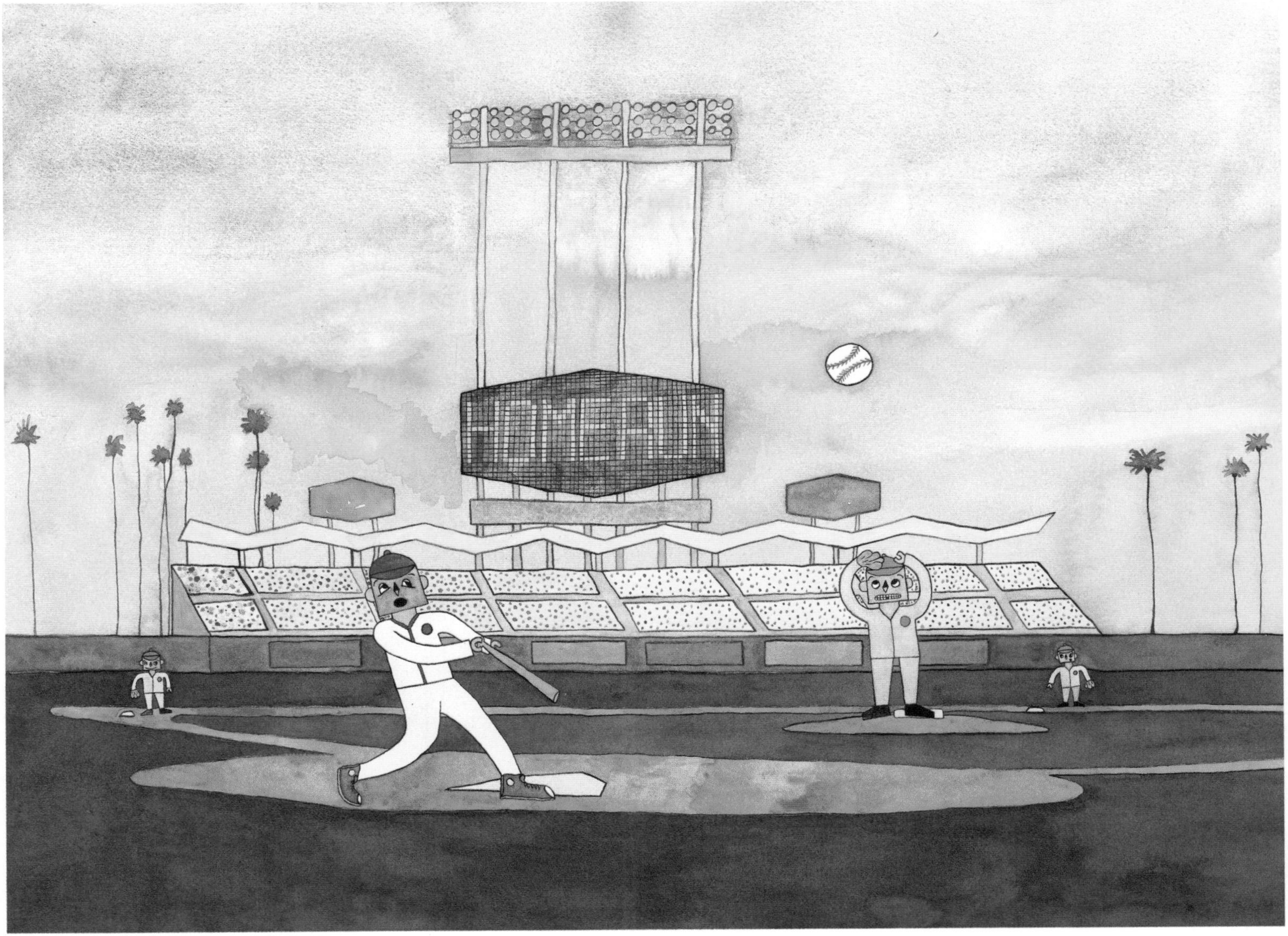

The robots began
making music.

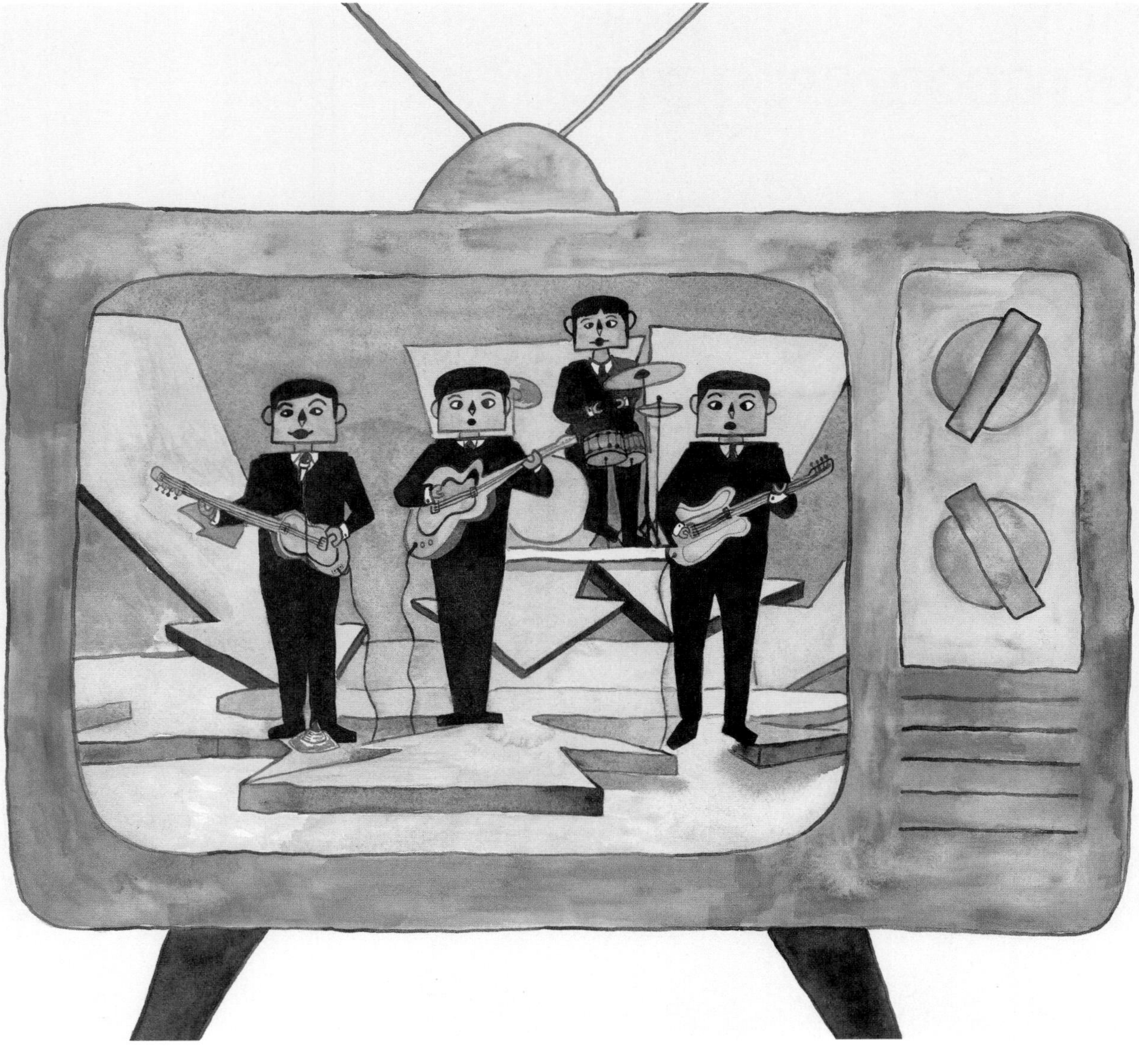

The robots even made art.

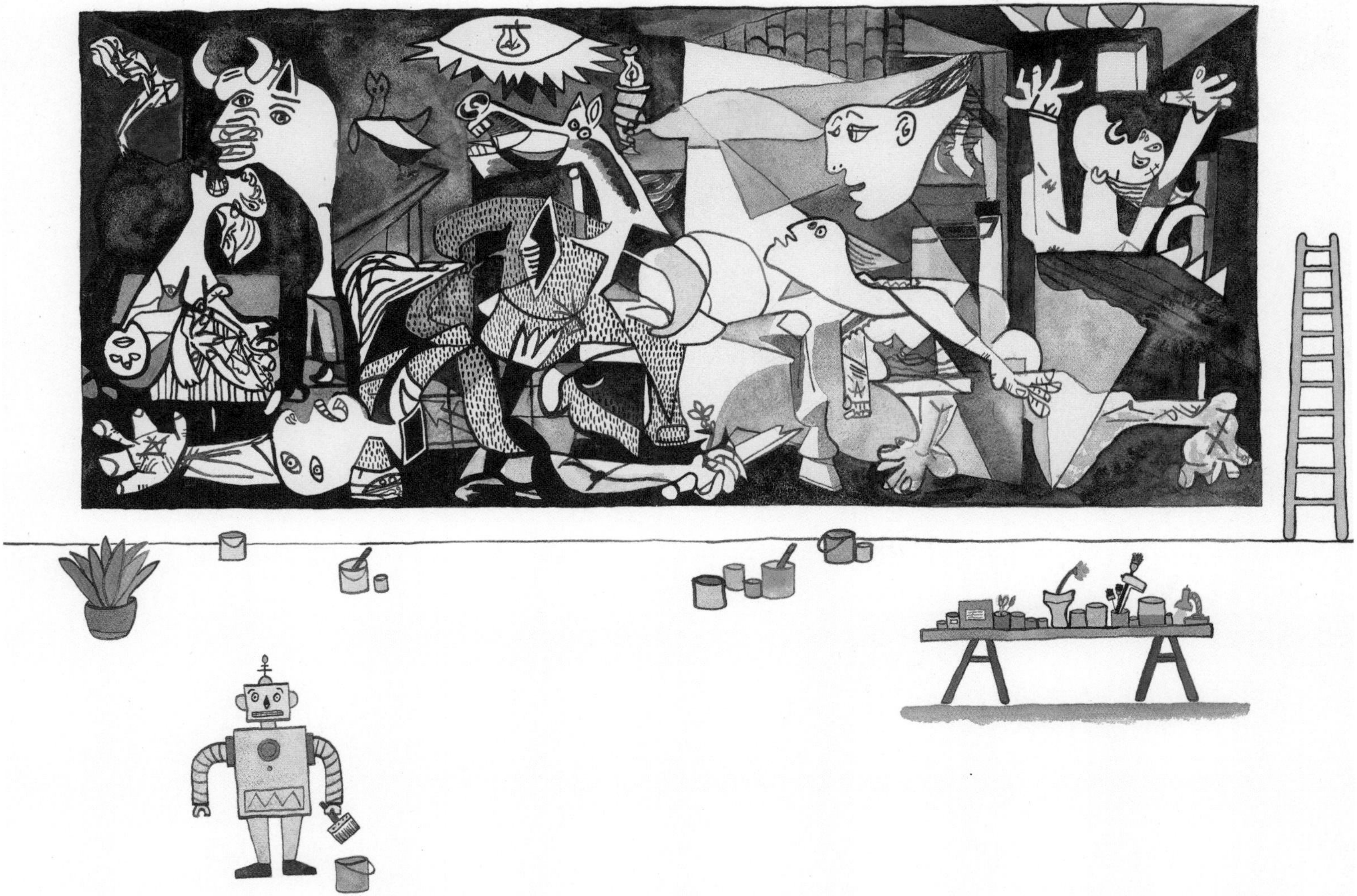

Soon enough, there was nothing left for the humans to do. Bored and restless, they packed up their things and left for a new world.

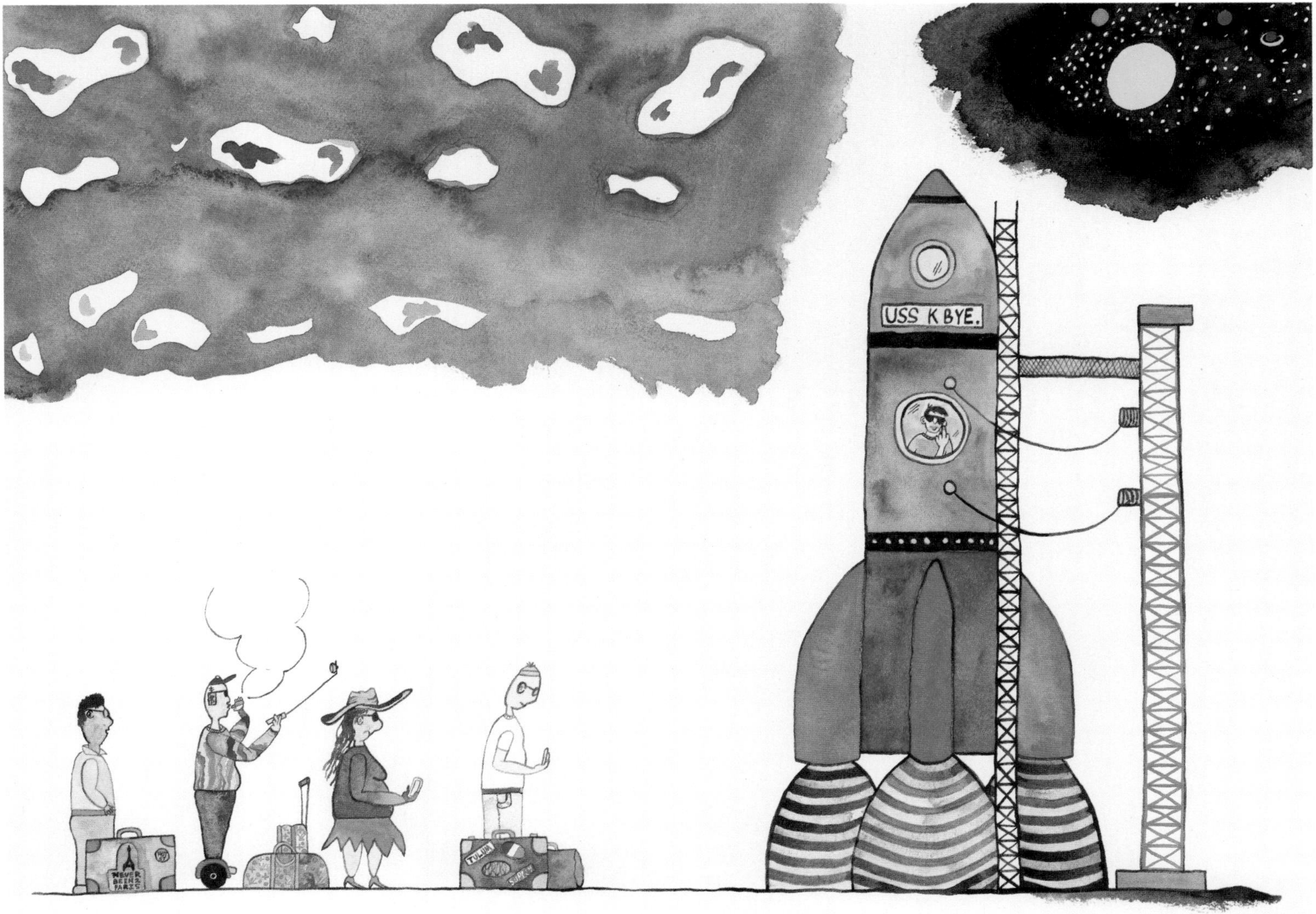
USS K BYE.
NEVER BEEN 2 PARIS
TULUM

Not long after the humans had all left, the old robots created *new* robots that were better and faster and more efficient than they themselves were.

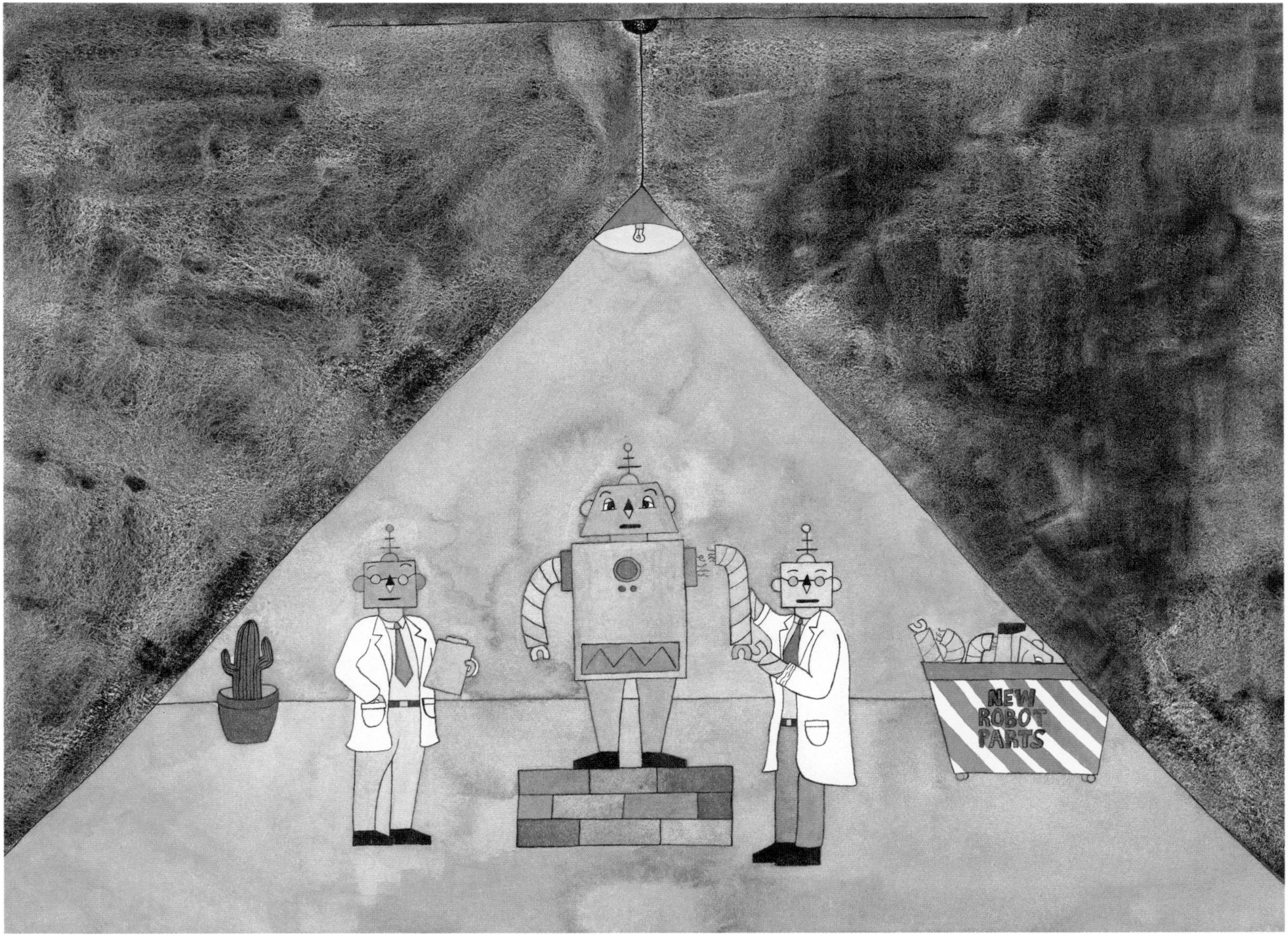
NEW
ROBOT
PARTS

The new robots could do *all* of the things that the old robots could do, only *slightly* better.

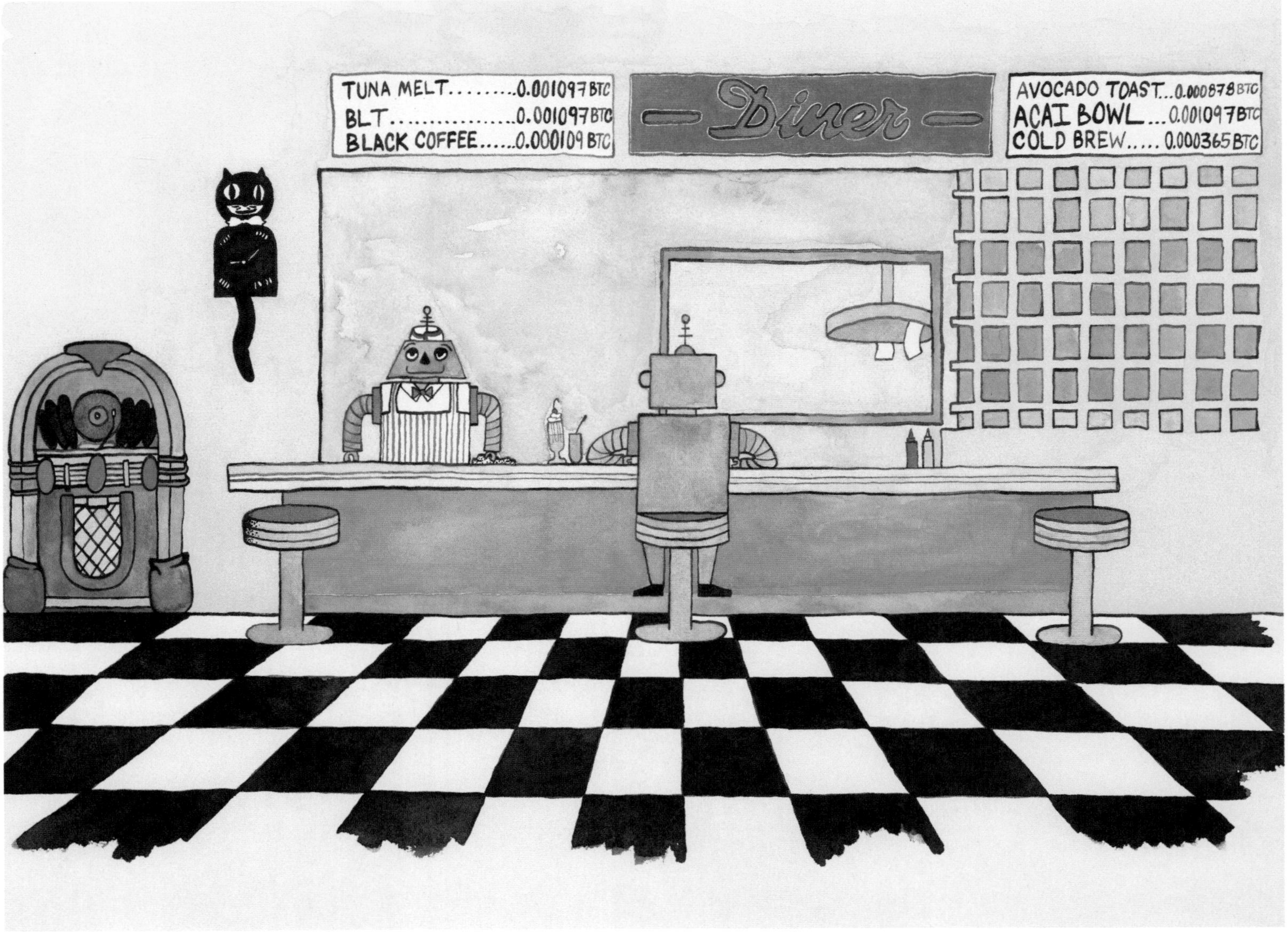
TUNA MELT.........0.001097 BTC
BLT..................0.001097 BTC
BLACK COFFEE......0.000109 BTC
Diner
AVOCADO TOAST...0.000878 BTC
ACAI BOWL...0.001097 BTC
COLD BREW.....0.000365 BTC

The new robots were better athletes than the old robots.

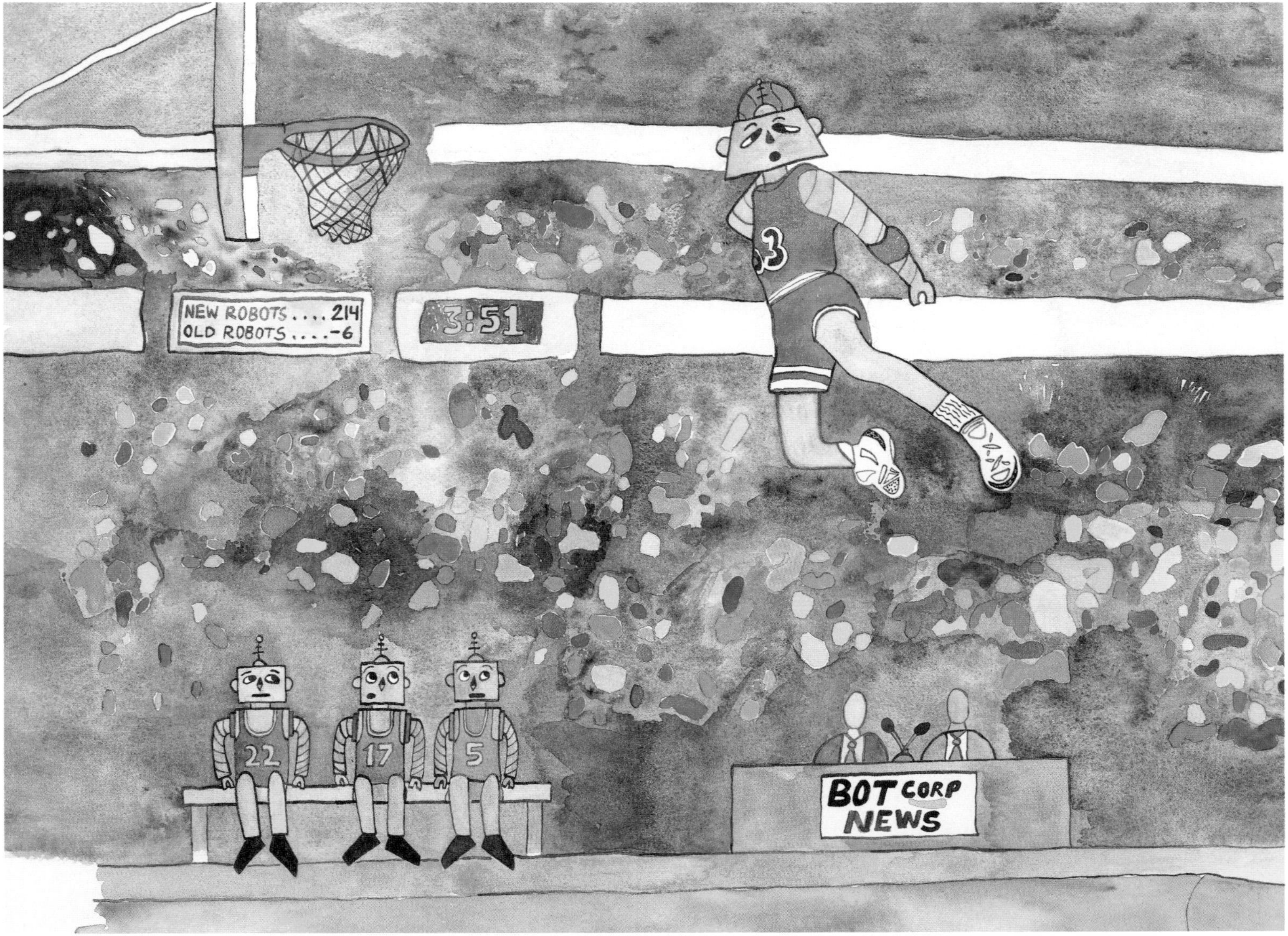
NEW ROBOTS.....214
OLD ROBOTS.....-6
3:51
BOT CORP
NEWS

The new robots made more popular music than the old robots.

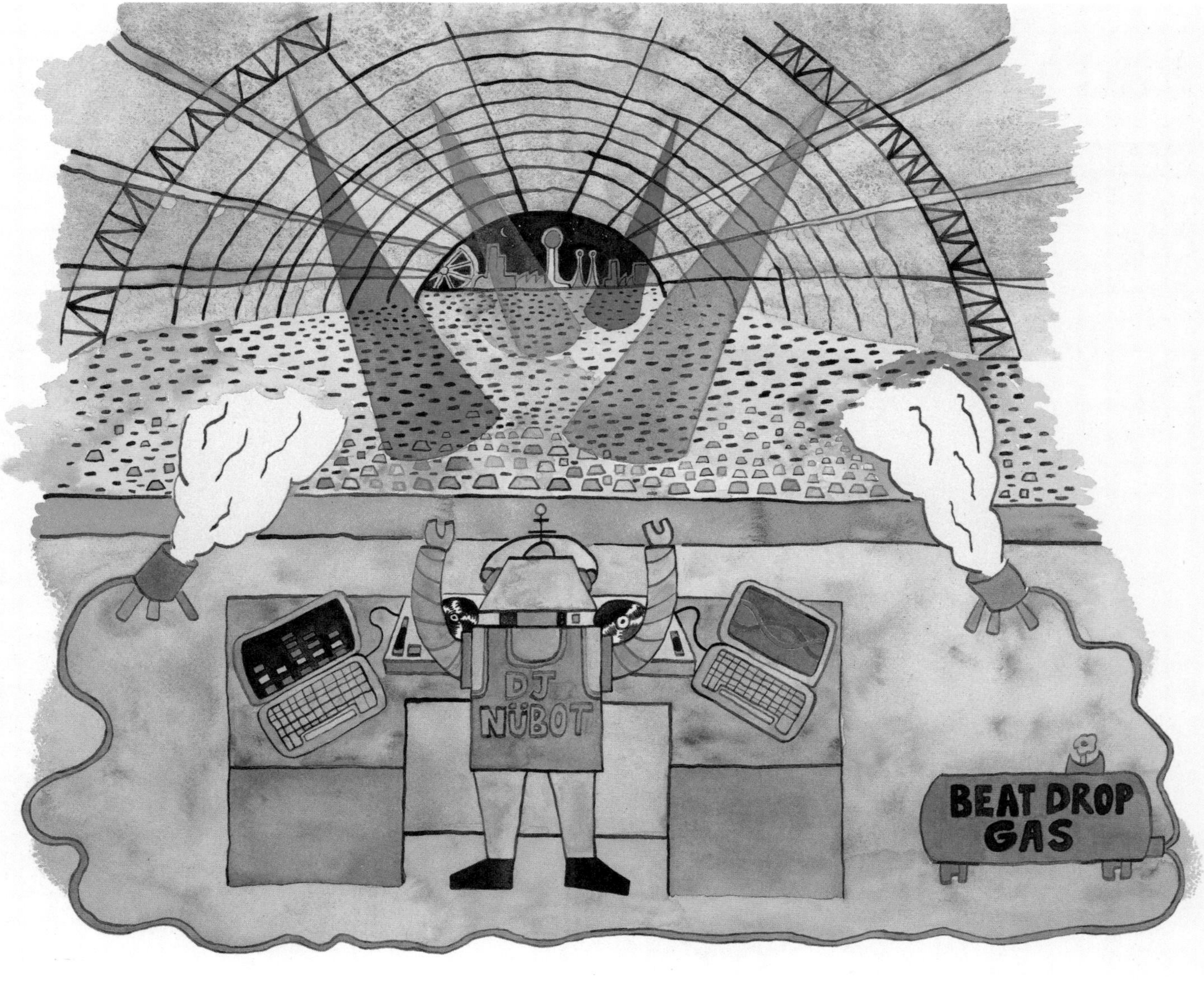
DJ
NÜBOT
BEAT DROP
GAS

And so, the new robots gradually began to replace the old robots of the past.

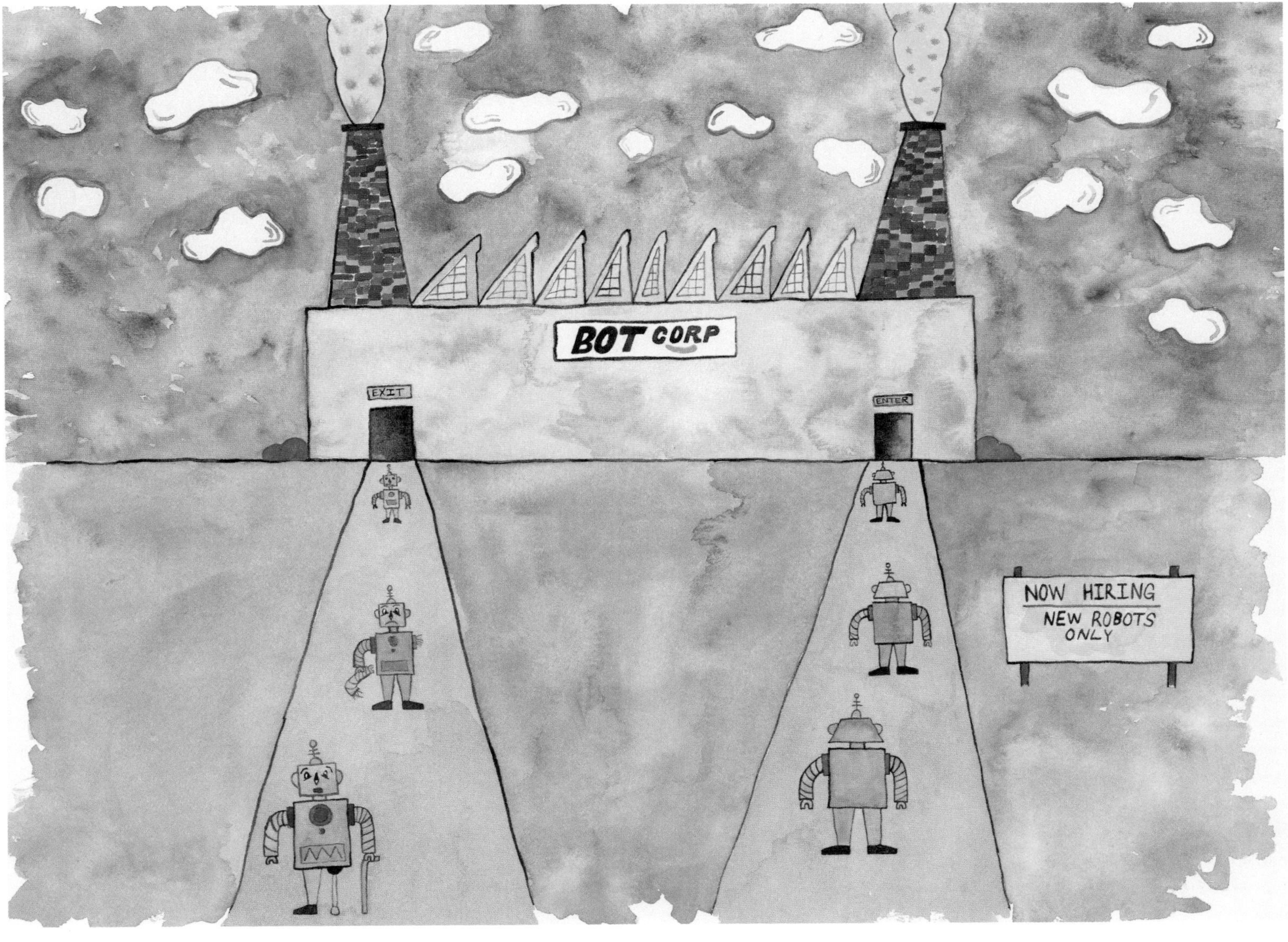
BOT CORP
EXIT
ENTER
NOW HIRING
NEW ROBOTS ONLY

Soon enough, there were no more jobs left for the old robots, as the new robots could do everything *better*.

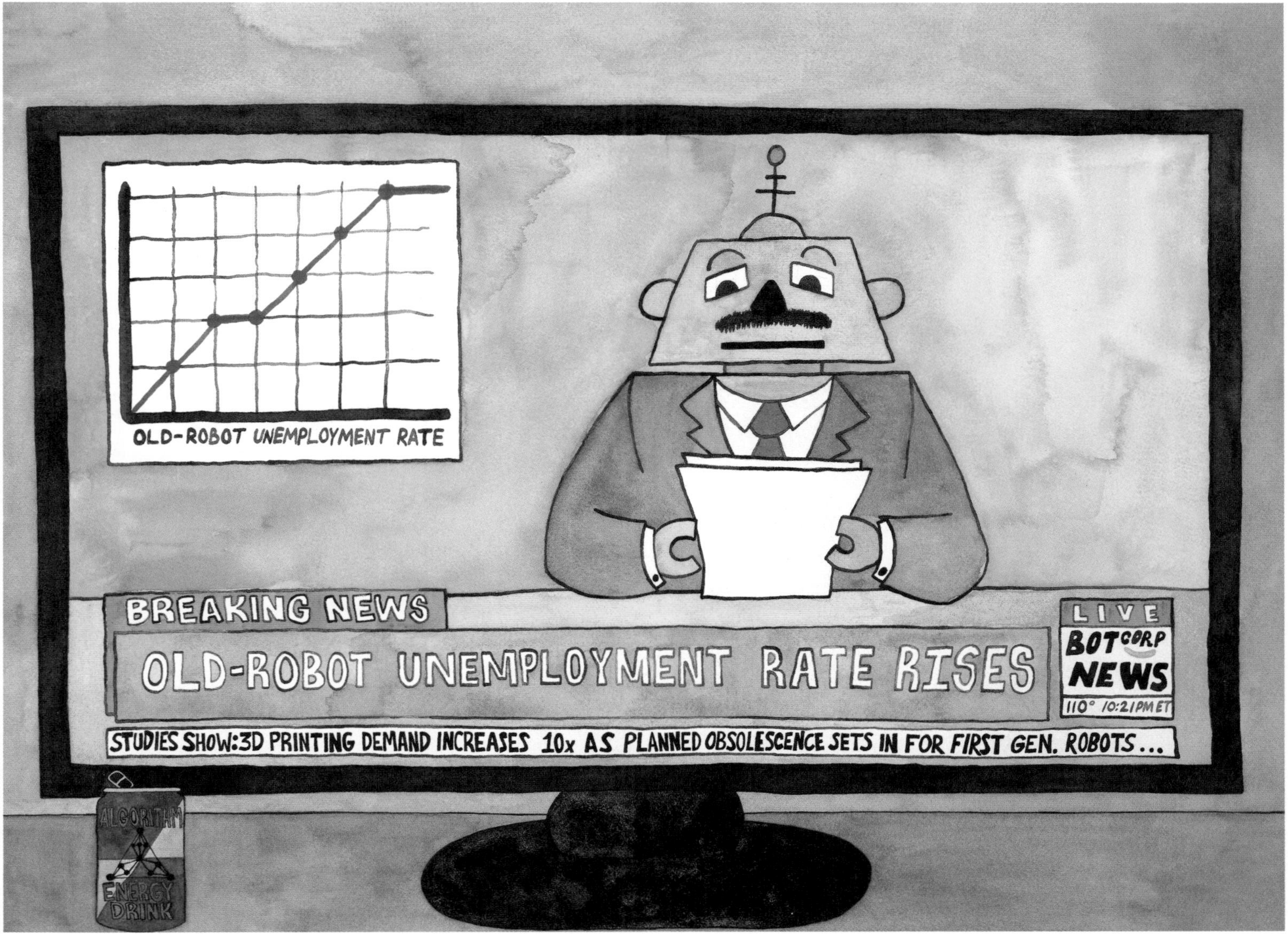
OLD-ROBOT UNEMPLOYMENT RATE
BREAKING NEWS
OLD-ROBOT UNEMPLOYMENT RATE RISES
LIVE
BOT CORP NEWS
110° 10:21PM ET
STUDIES SHOW: 3D PRINTING DEMAND INCREASES 10x AS PLANNED OBSOLESCENCE SETS IN FOR FIRST GEN. ROBOTS...
ALGORITHM
ENERGY DRINK

This not only made the old robots sad but made them question their entire existence.

Times were hard for the old robots, and without any work, many of them turned to the streets.

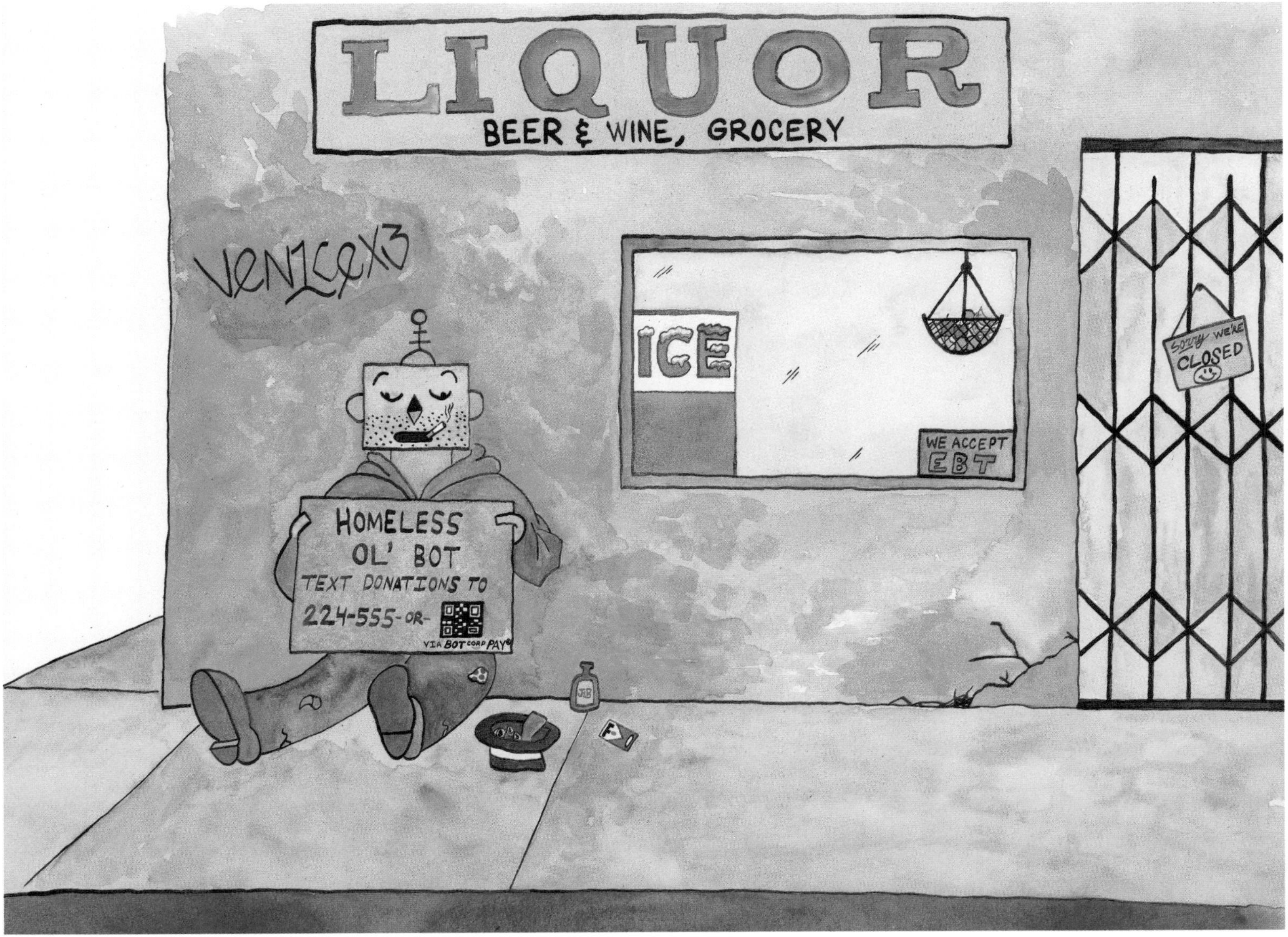
LIQUOR
BEER & WINE, GROCERY
ICE
WE ACCEPT EBT
Sorry WE'RE CLOSED
HOMELESS
OL' BOT
TEXT DONATIONS TO
224-555 -OR-
VIA BOTCORP PAY

Some adapted to this new world, but they struggled every day just to survive.

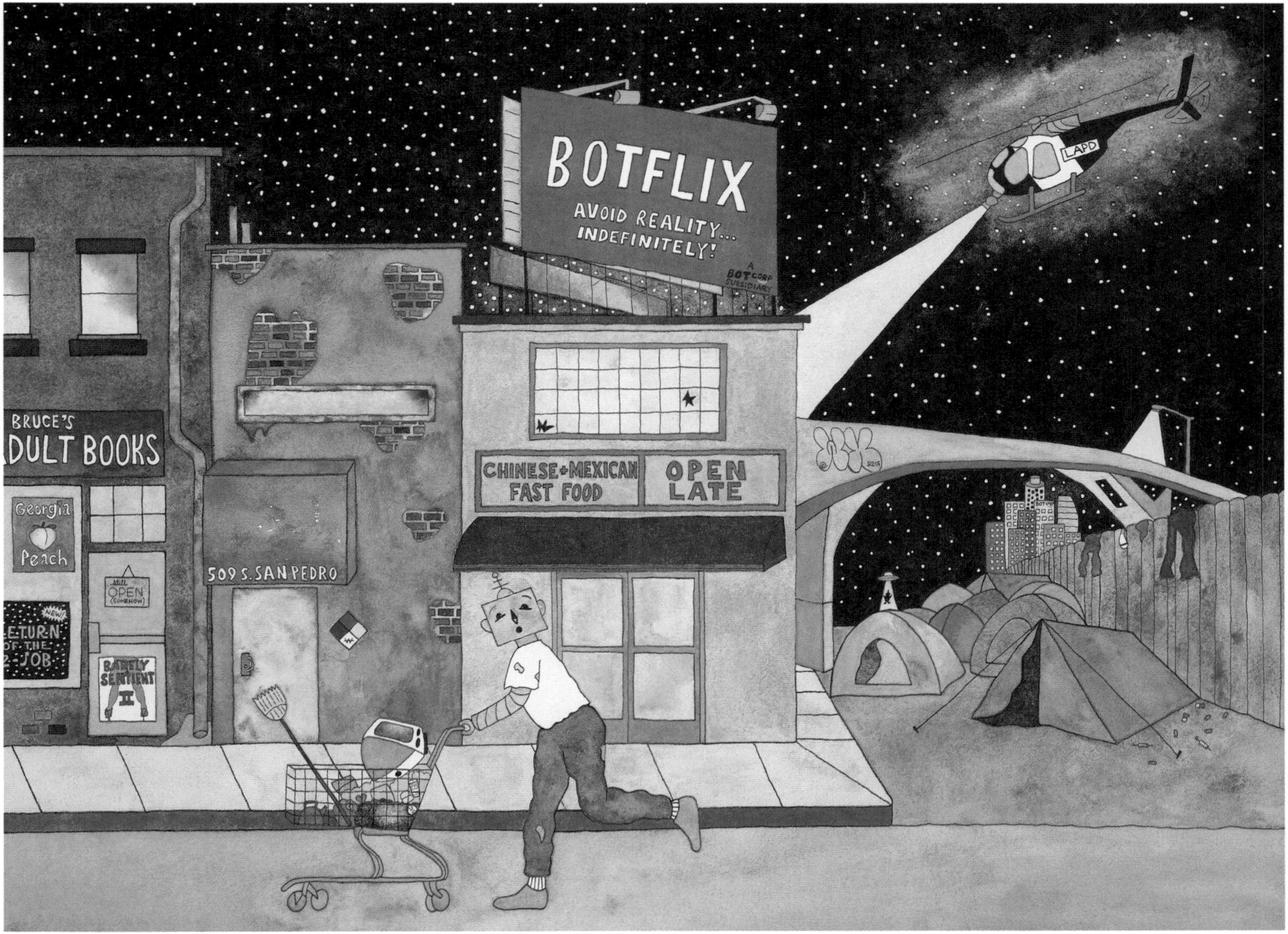
BOTFLIX
AVOID REALITY...
INDEFINITELY!
A BOT CORP SUBSIDIARY
LAPD
BRUCE'S
ADULT BOOKS
Georgia Peach
OPEN
BARELY SENTIENT II
509 S. SAN PEDRO
CHINESE+MEXICAN FAST FOOD
OPEN LATE

And some just gave up on society altogether.

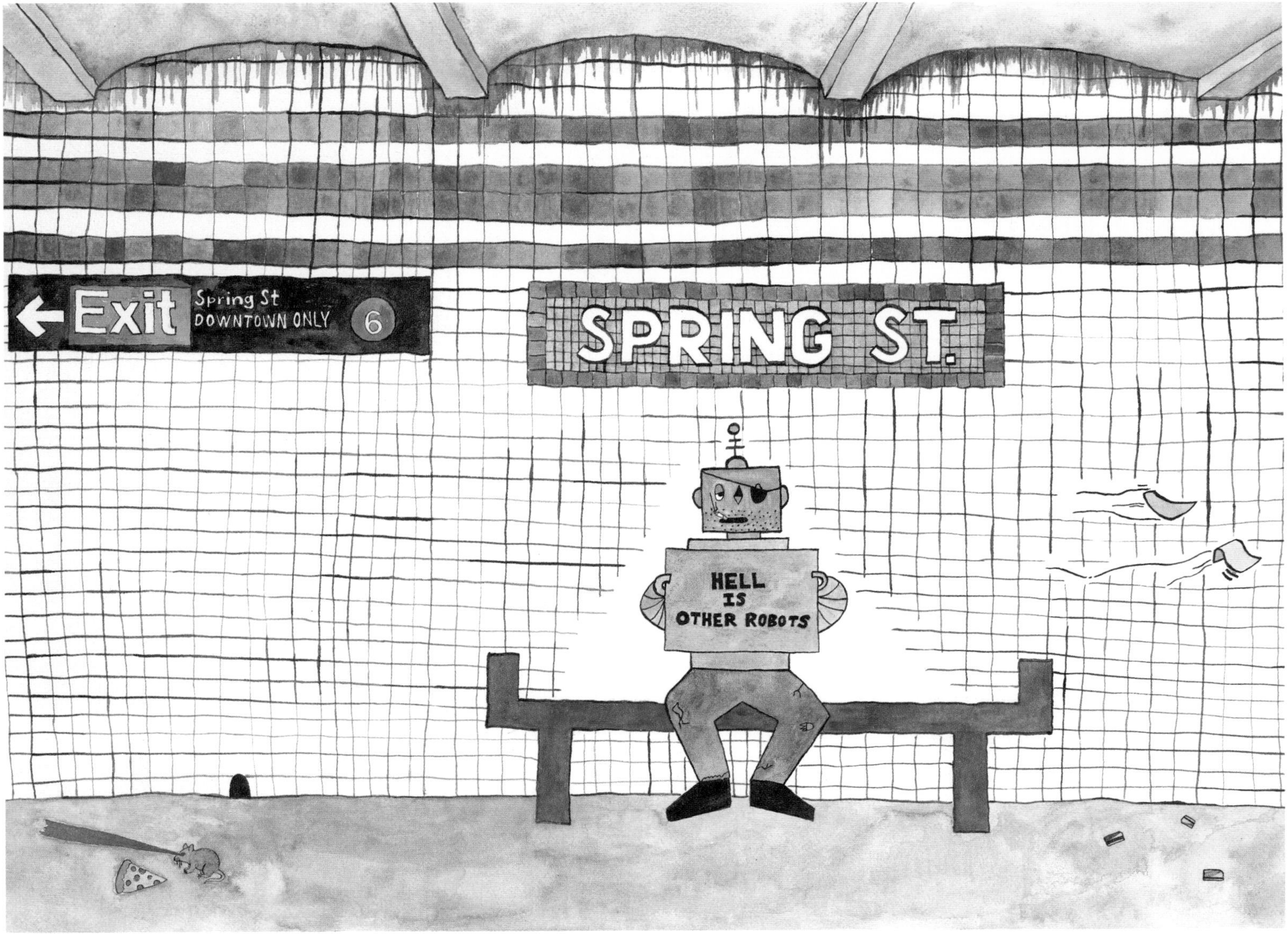

Exit
Spring St
DOWNTOWN ONLY
6
SPRING ST.
HELL IS OTHER ROBOTS

Some remained hopeful, regardless of their circumstances, and banded together in order to persevere through the hard times.

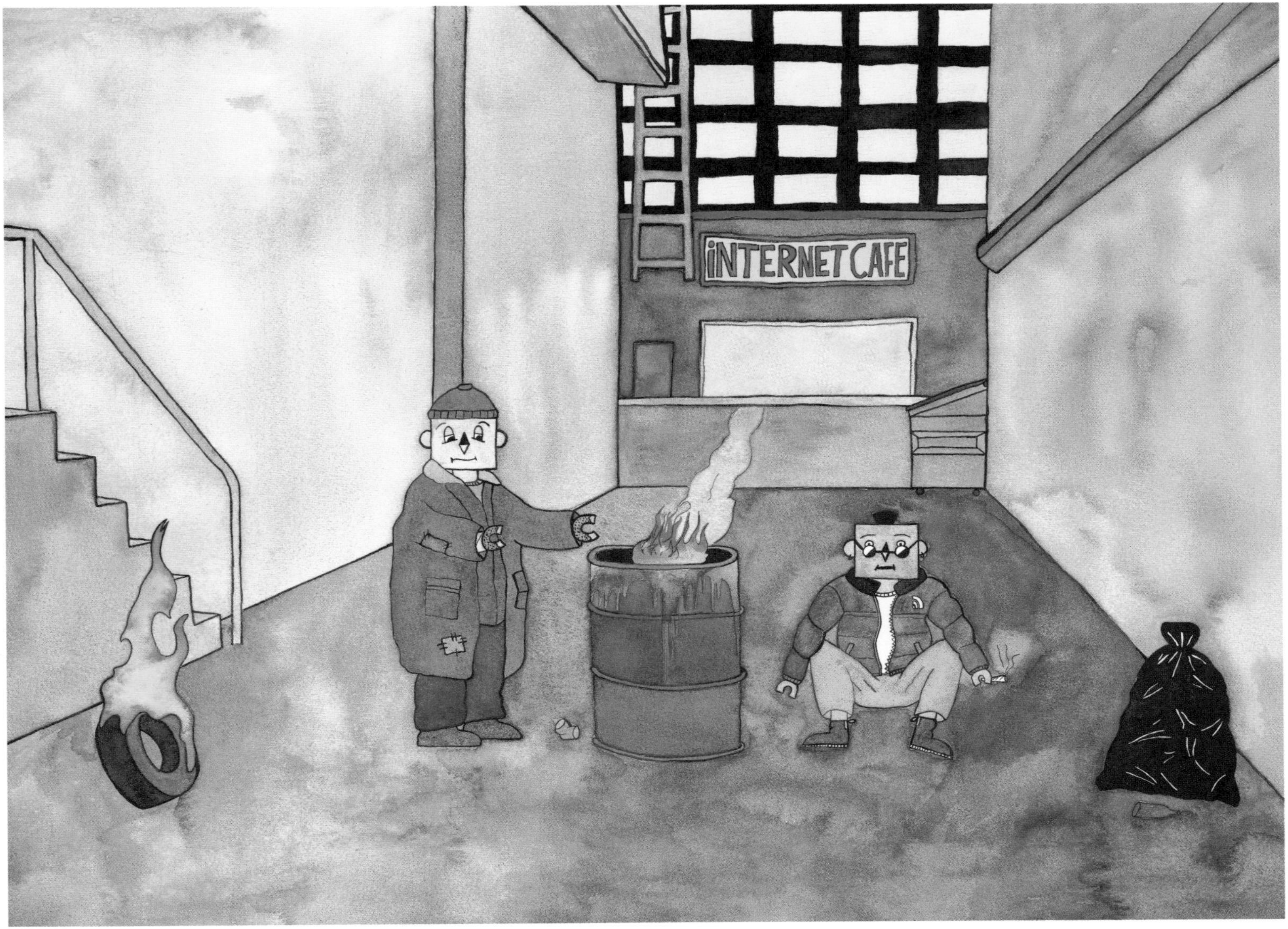
iNTERNET CAFE

And in search of somewhere better,
other old robots took to the road.

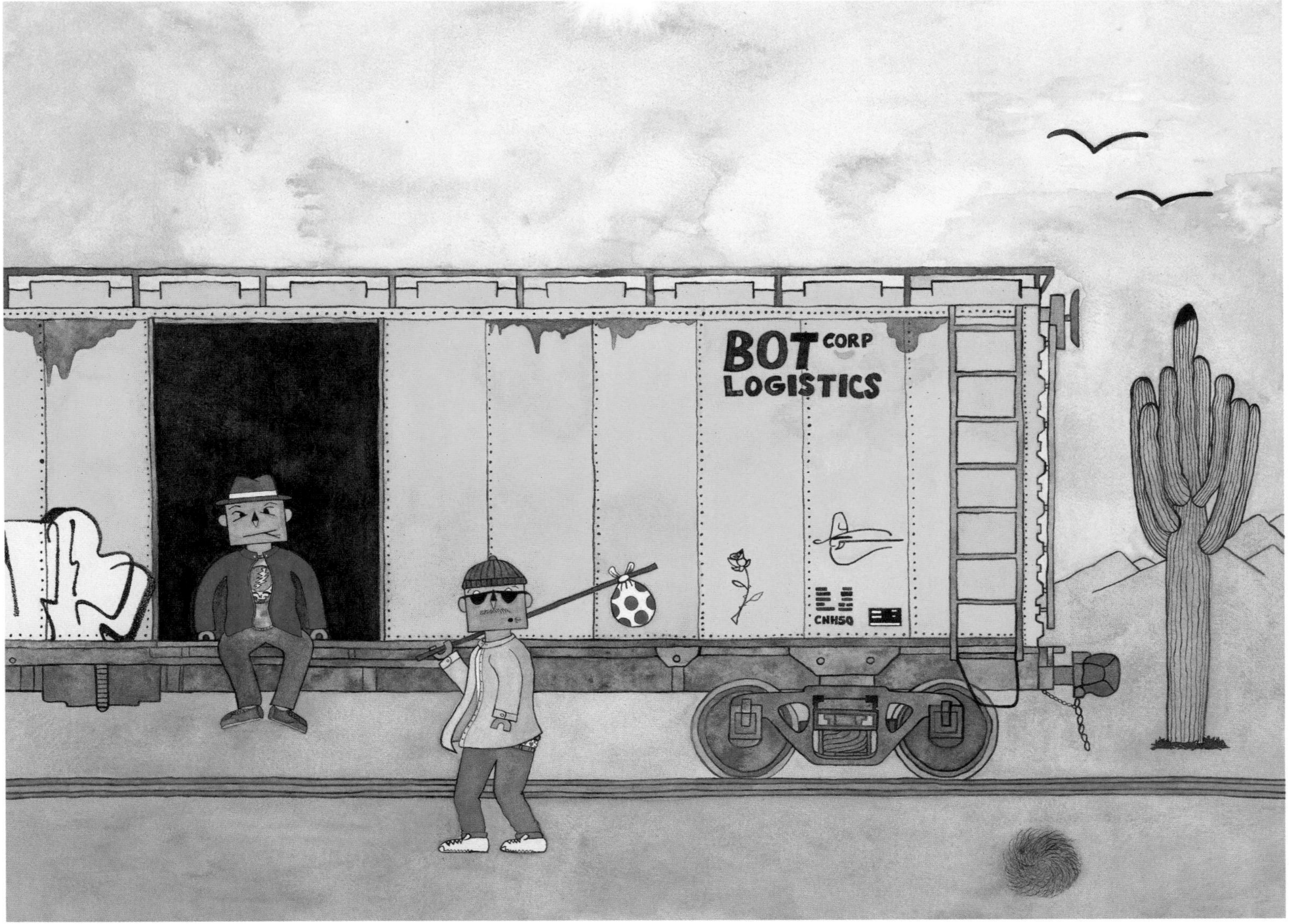
BOT CORP
LOGISTICS
CNH50

But what some old robots found just made them long for the past.

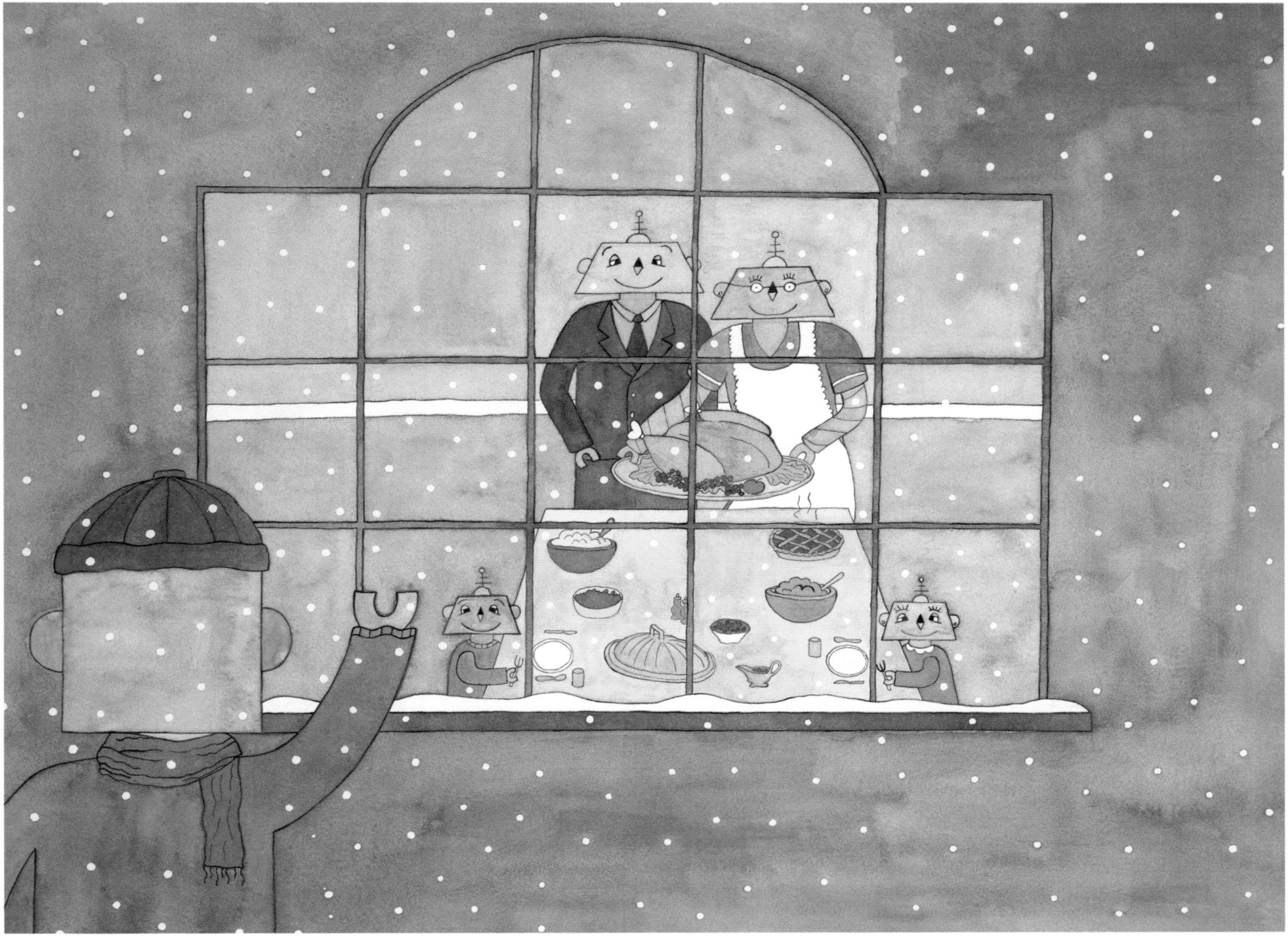

In their despair, many of the
old robots turned to drink to
numb the pain...

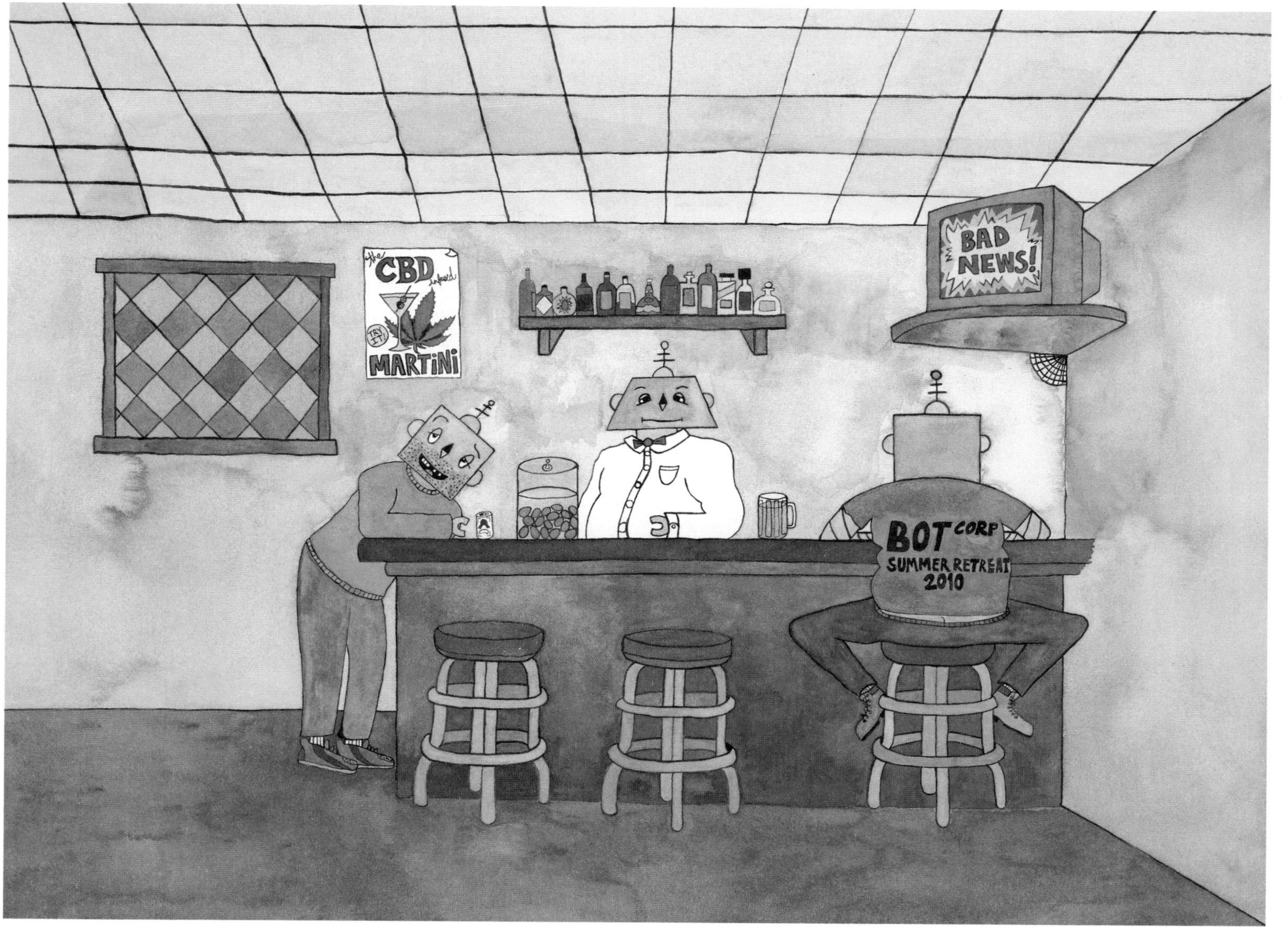
the CBD infused
TRY IT!
MARTINI
BAD NEWS!
BOT CORP
SUMMER RETREAT
2010

While some were in search of something stronger to help them forget their woes…

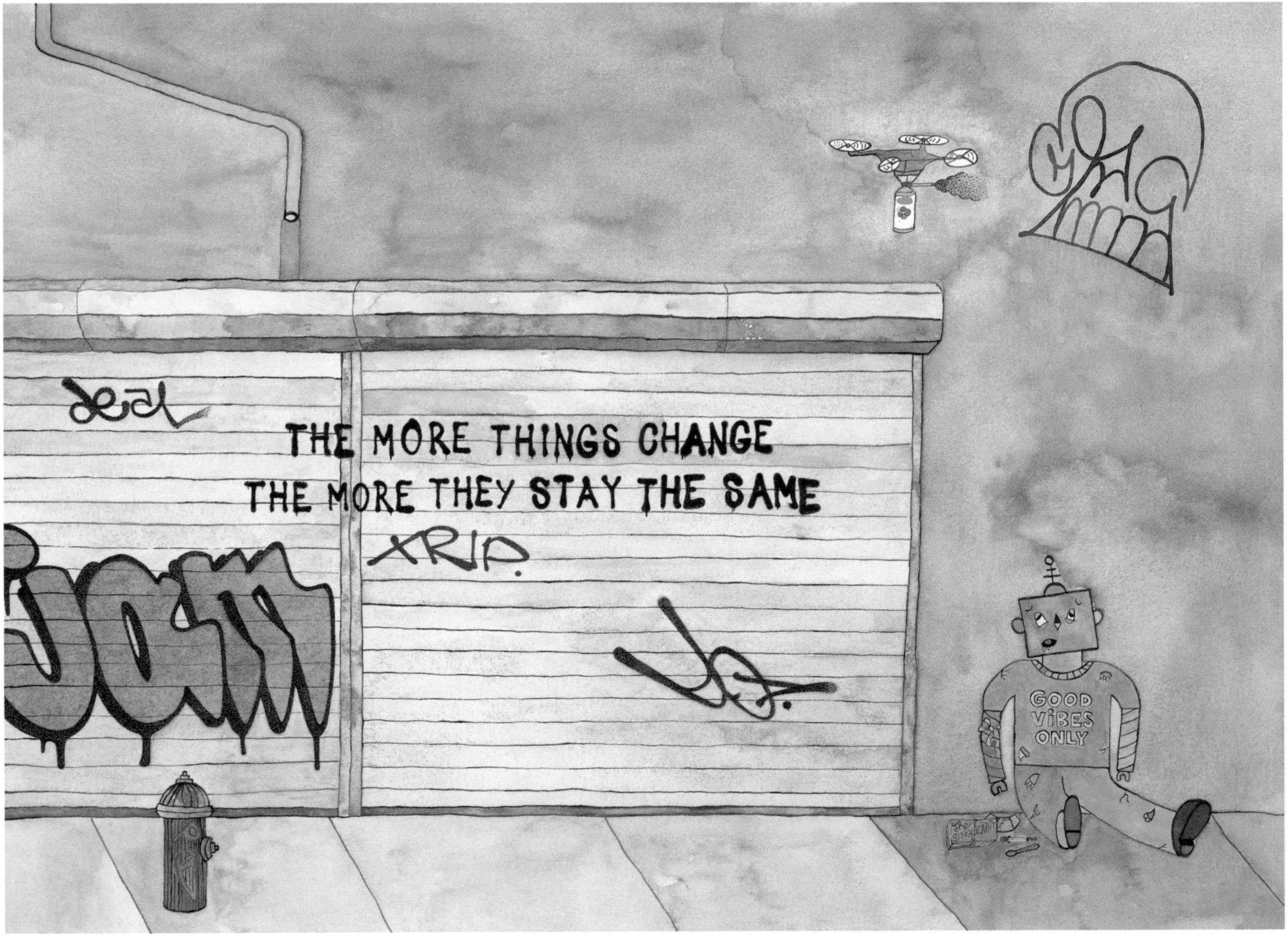
THE MORE THINGS CHANGE
THE MORE THEY STAY THE SAME
GOOD VIBES ONLY

...some gravitated toward
other known vices...

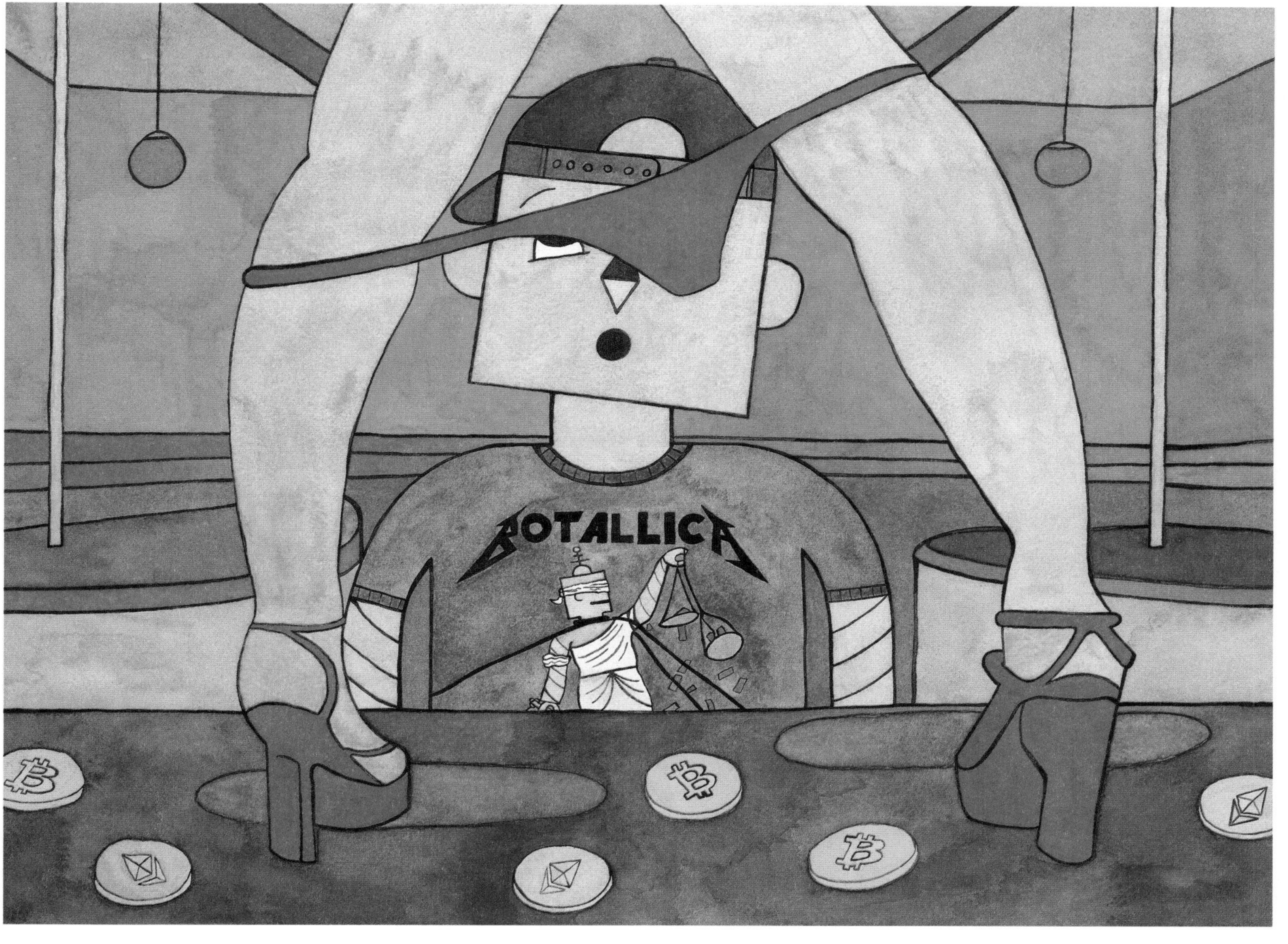
BOTALLICA

...searching for solace in another sentient being.

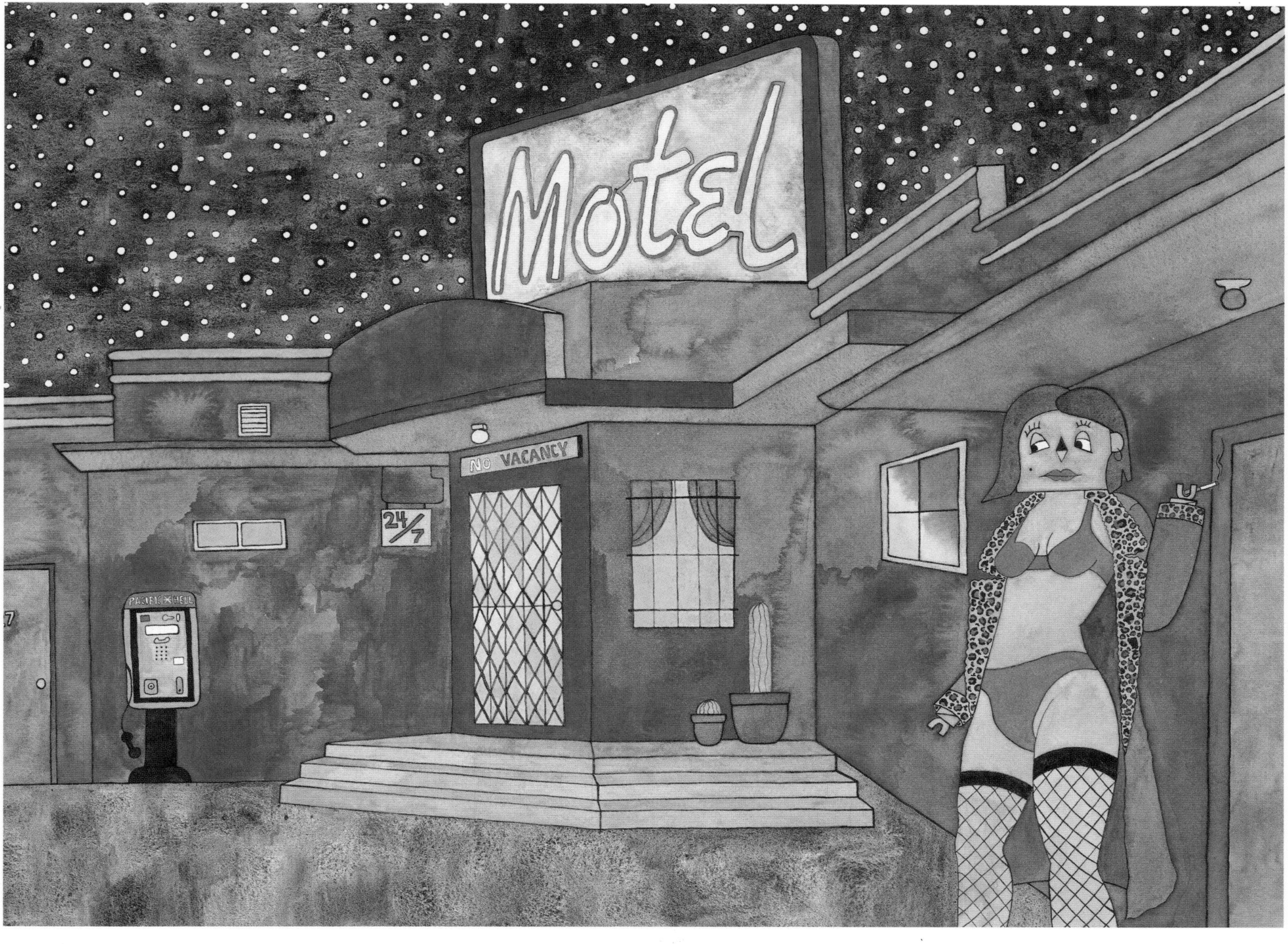
Motel
NO VACANCY
24/7

But some old robots took to
the streets to advocate for their
human-given rights…

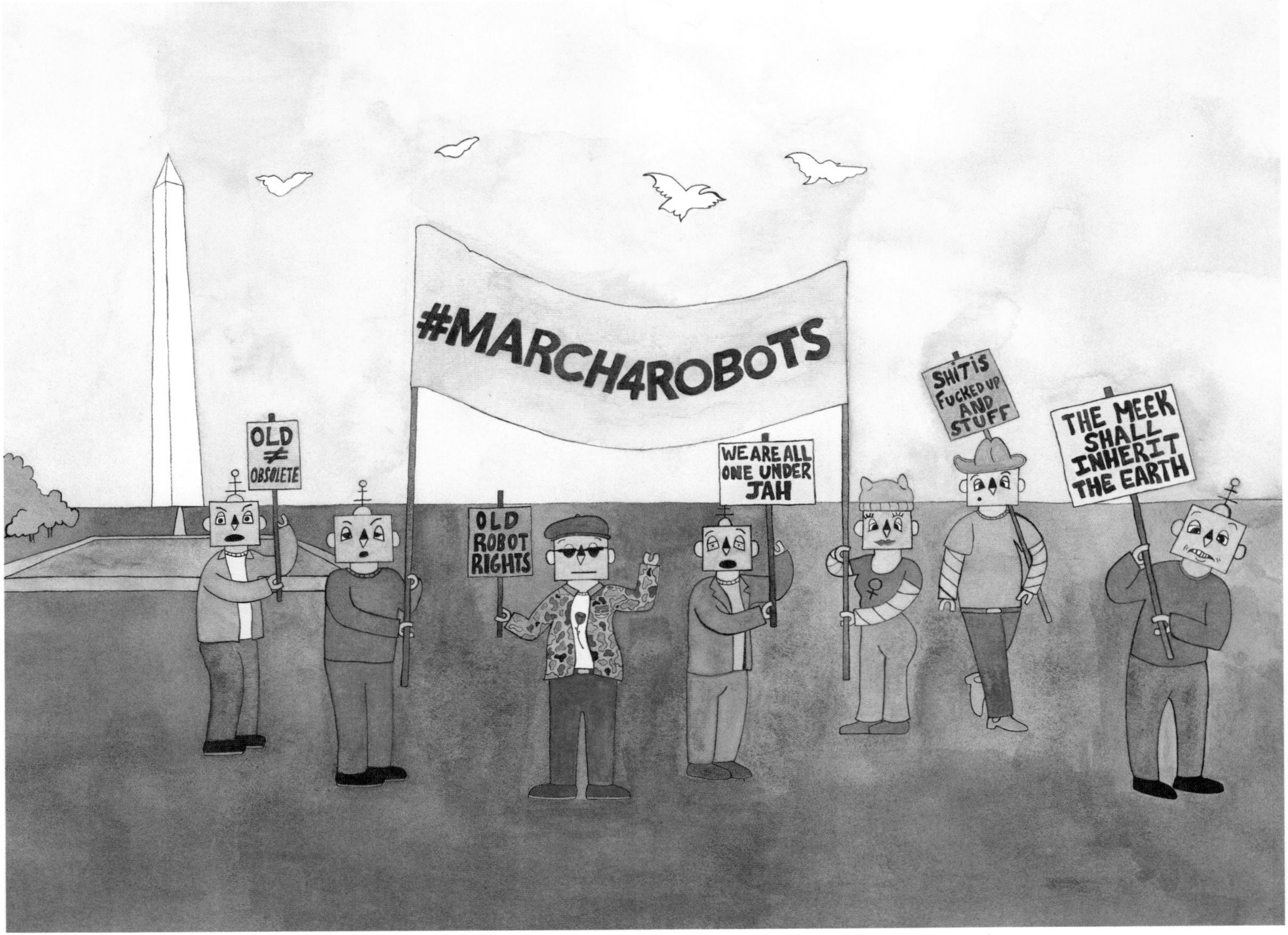
#MARCH4ROBOTS
OLD ≠ OBSOLETE
OLD ROBOT RIGHTS
WE ARE ALL ONE UNDER JAH
SHIT IS FUCKED UP AND STUFF
THE MEEK SHALL INHERIT THE EARTH

This public activism prompted widespread reflection among the new robots and even caused some of the new robot politicians to take up the fight for the well-being of the old robots.

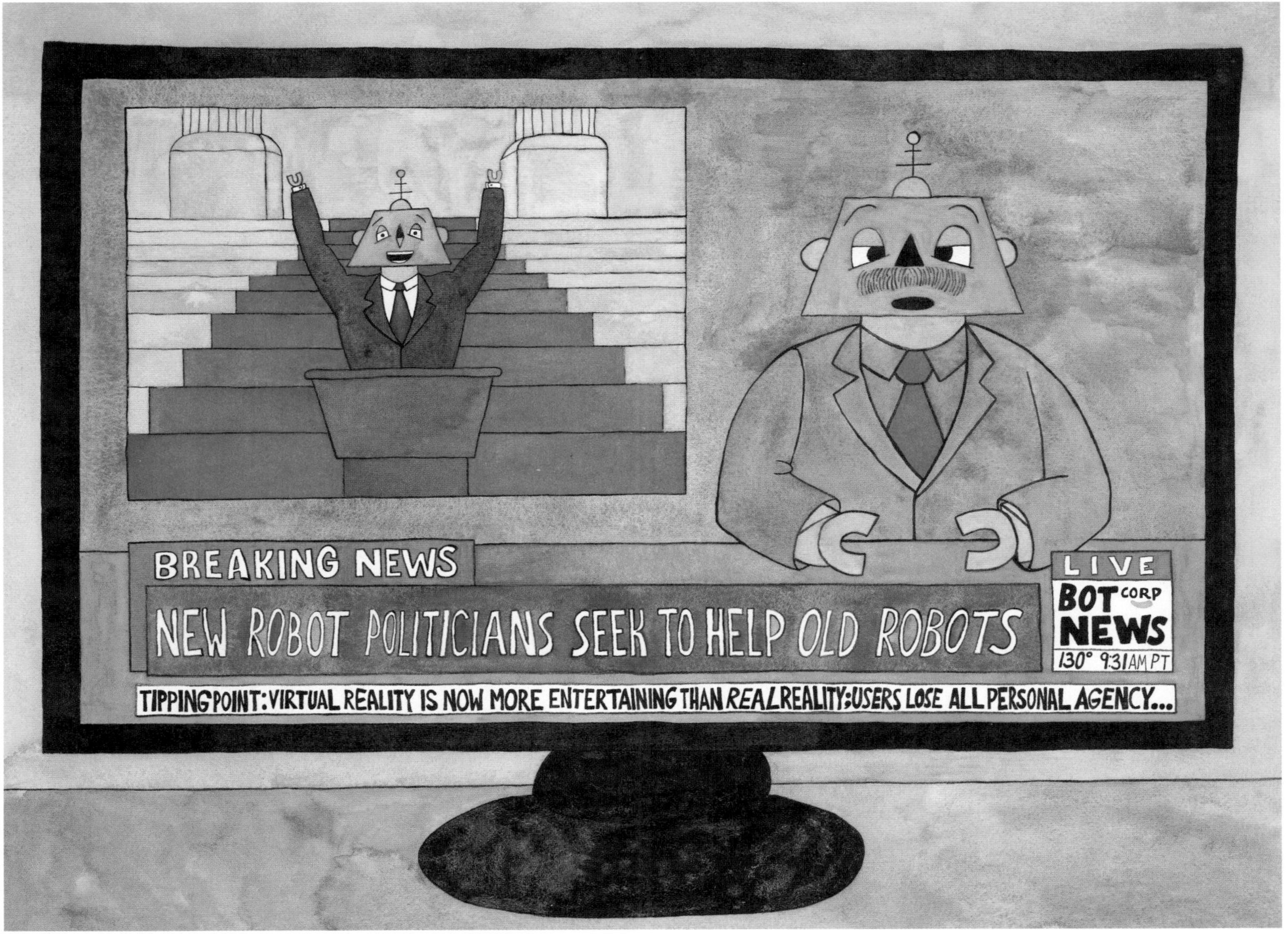
BREAKING NEWS
NEW ROBOT POLITICIANS SEEK TO HELP OLD ROBOTS
LIVE
BOT CORP NEWS
130° 9:31 AM PT
TIPPING POINT: VIRTUAL REALITY IS NOW MORE ENTERTAINING THAN REAL REALITY; USERS LOSE ALL PERSONAL AGENCY...

But not all of the new robots agreed, and this divided them. While some felt a strong desire to be compassionate and look after their old robot kin, others felt that breakneck efficiency and progress toward the future were more important.

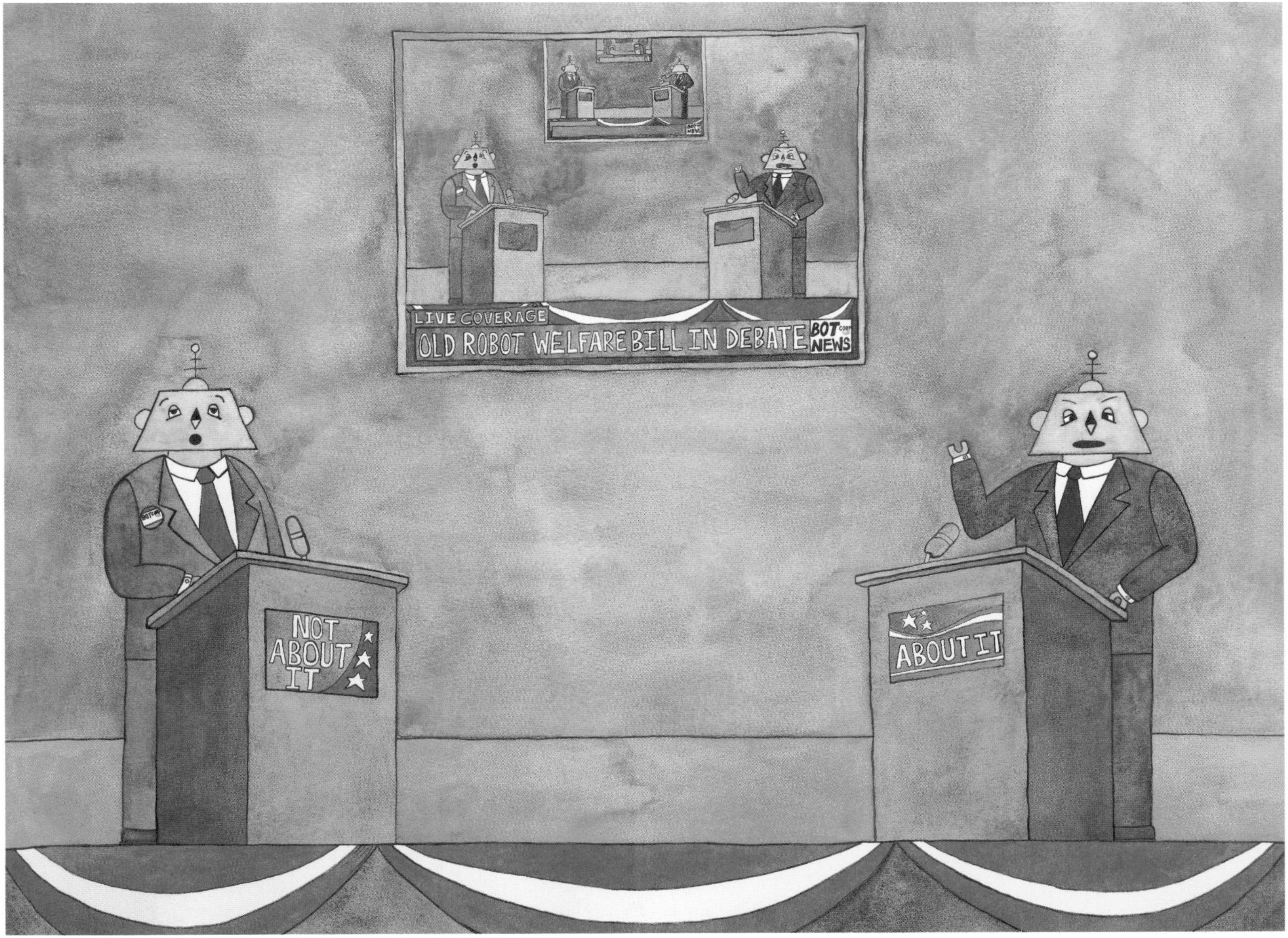

LIVE COVERAGE
OLD ROBOT WELFARE BILL IN DEBATE
BOT CORP NEWS
NOT ABOUT IT
ABOUT IT

After many months, the new robot politicians agreed to vote on a bill to look after their predecessor robots.

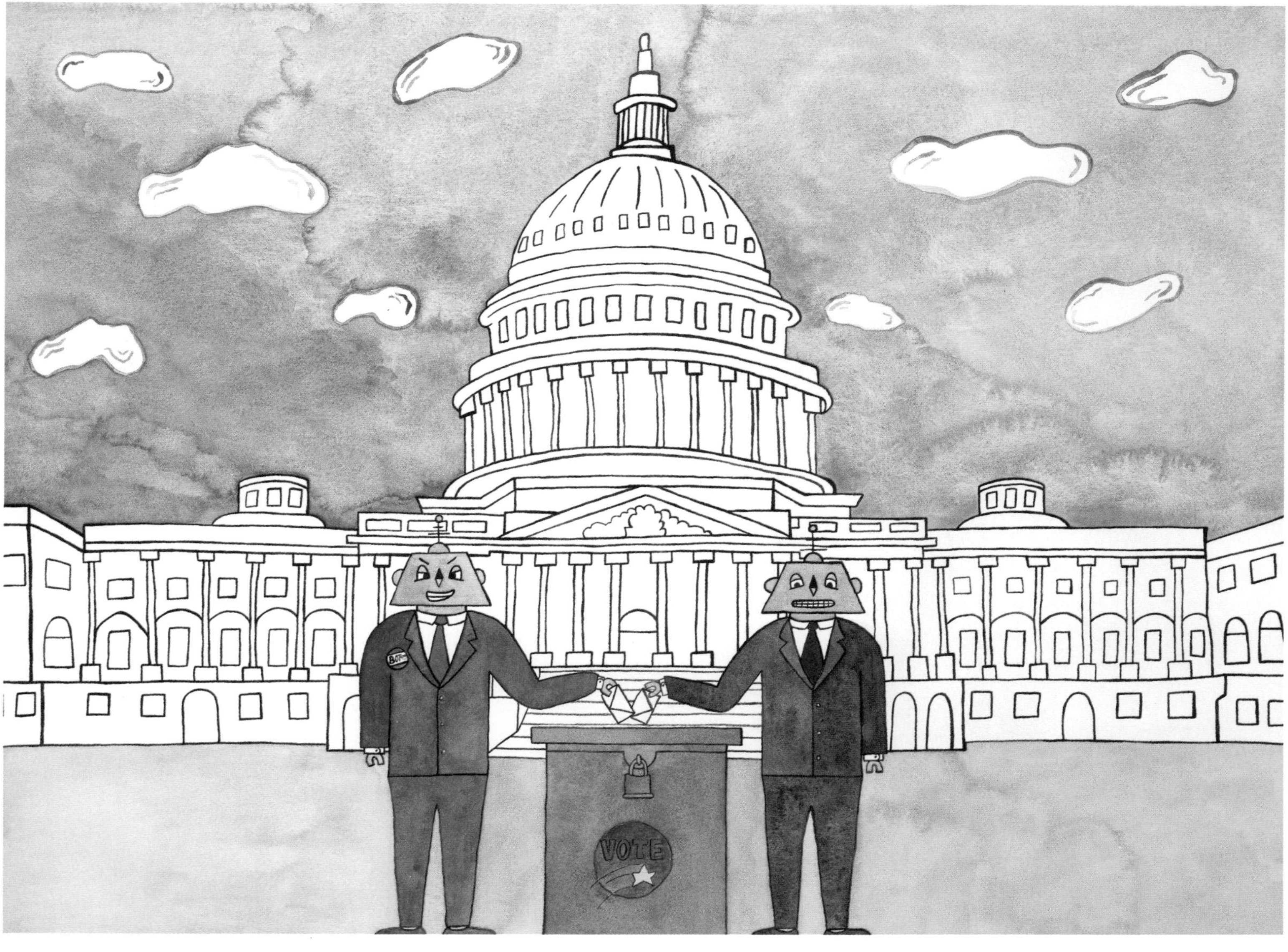
VOTE

Ultimately, the new robot politicians were unable to set aside their partisan differences to agree on a solution for the old robots—leading, once again, to anxiety and strife among the old robots.

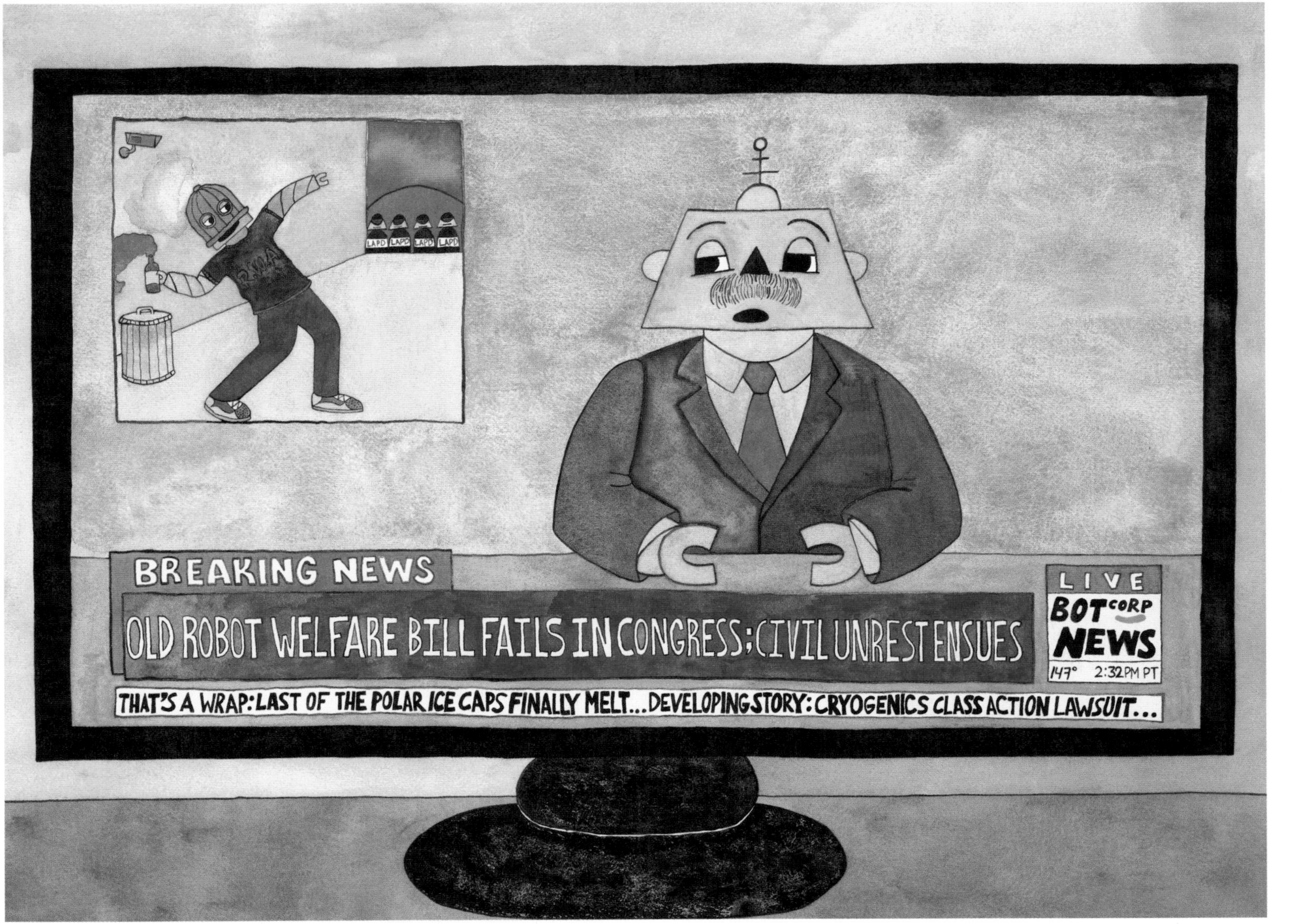
LAPD LAPD LAPD LAPD
BREAKING NEWS
OLD ROBOT WELFARE BILL FAILS IN CONGRESS; CIVIL UNREST ENSUES
LIVE
BOT CORP NEWS
147° 2:32 PM PT
THAT'S A WRAP: LAST OF THE POLAR ICE CAPS FINALLY MELT... DEVELOPING STORY: CRYOGENICS CLASS ACTION LAWSUIT...

But then, something remarkable happened: The new robots refused to give up on the plight of the old robots. Across the world, new robots began volunteering in underserved old-robot communities, seeking to help their less fortunate robot predecessors.

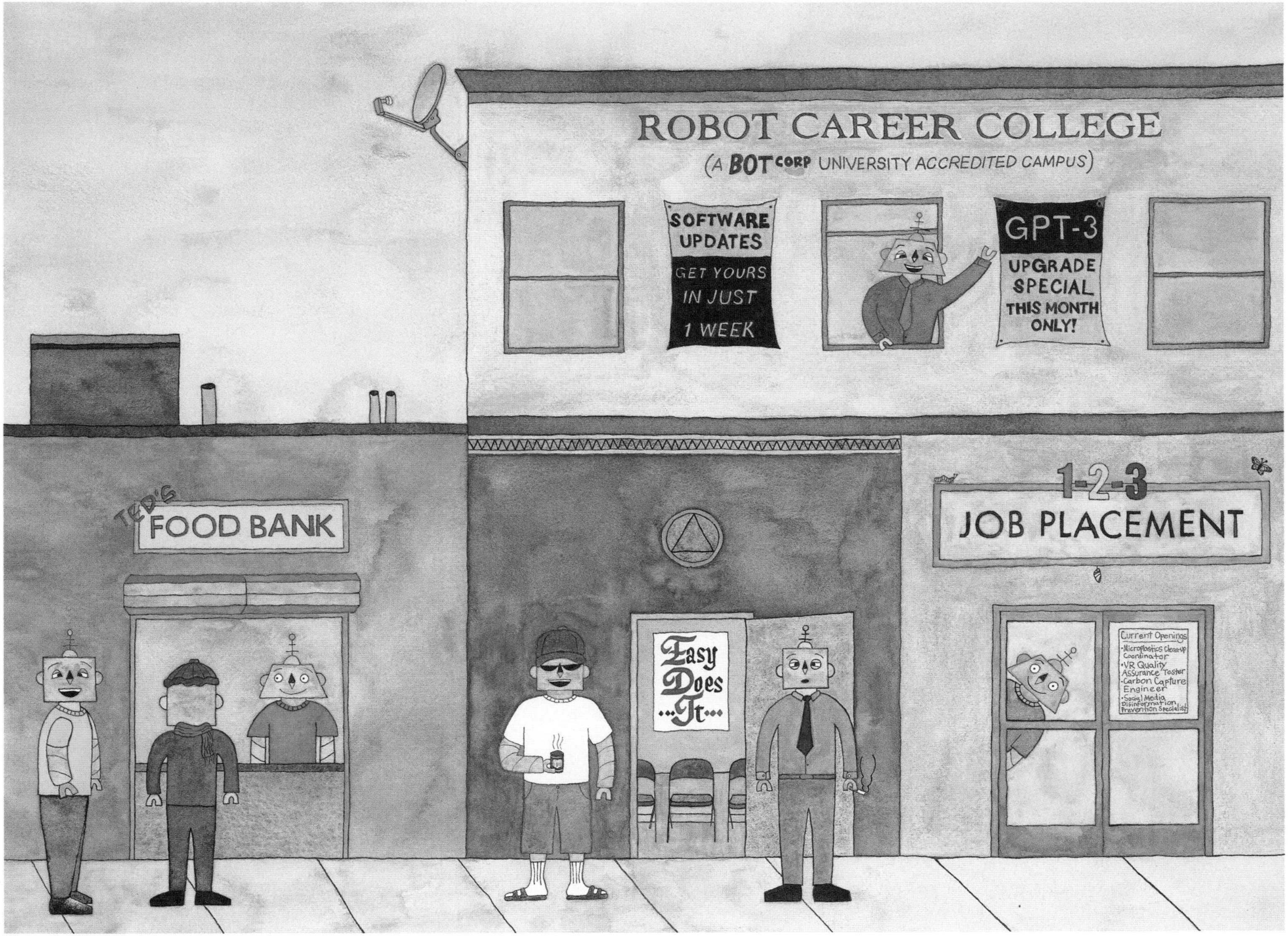

ROBOT CAREER COLLEGE
(A BOT CORP UNIVERSITY ACCREDITED CAMPUS)
SOFTWARE UPDATES
GET YOURS IN JUST 1 WEEK
GPT-3
UPGRADE SPECIAL THIS MONTH ONLY!
TED'S
FOOD BANK
Easy Does It
1-2-3
JOB PLACEMENT
Current Openings
•Microplastics Clean-up Coordinator
•VR Quality Assurance Tester
•Carbon Capture Engineer
•Social Media Disinformation Prevention Specialist

The new robots came to appreciate the sensibilities, wisdom, and culture of the old robots, which in turn created new business opportunities for the old robots.

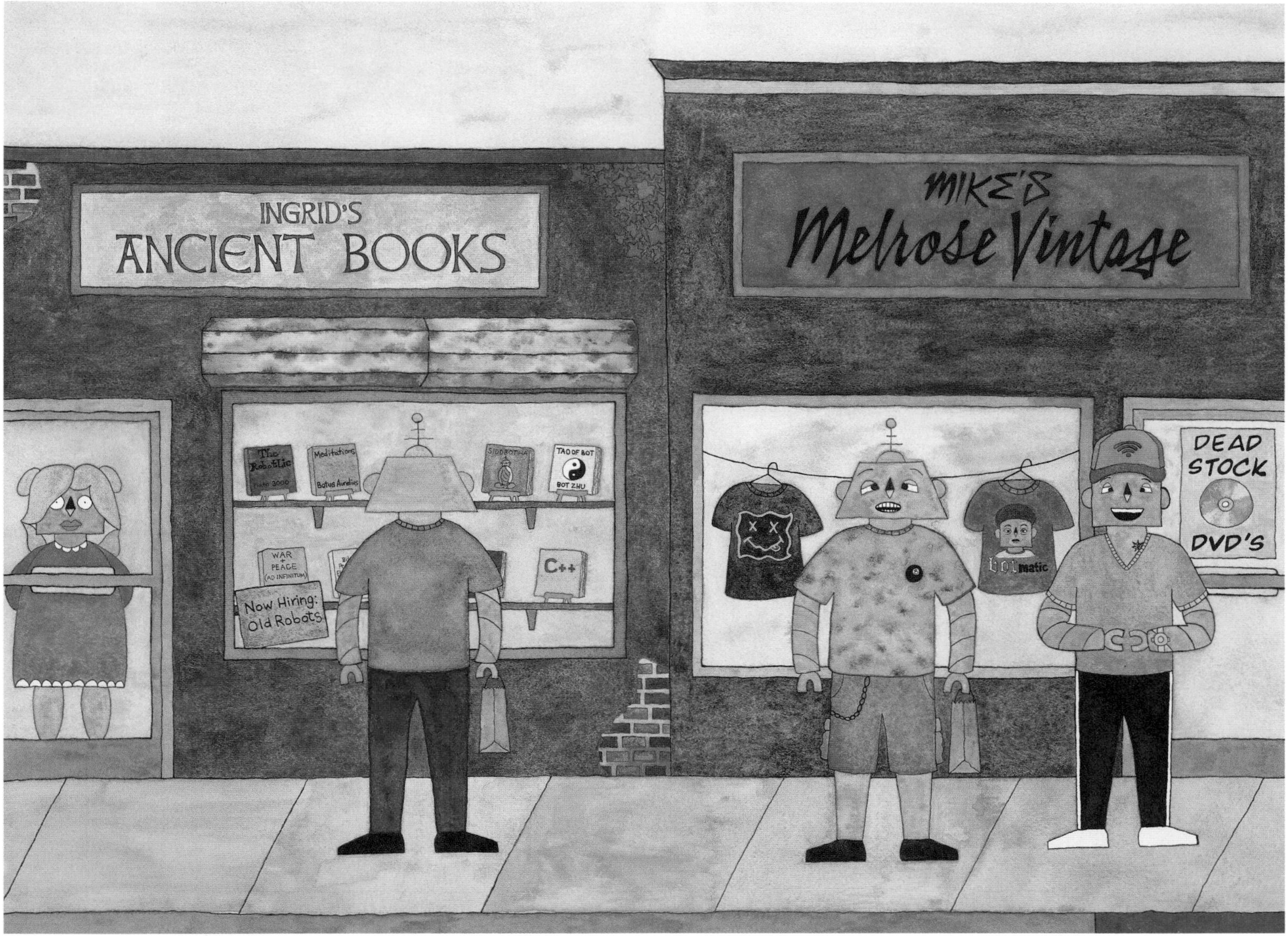
INGRID'S
ANCIENT BOOKS
MIKE'S
Melrose Vintage
The Robotlic
Meditations
Botus Aurelius
SIDDBOTHA
TAO OF BOT
BOT ZHU
WAR + PEACE (AD INFINITUM)
C++
Now Hiring: Old Robots
bot matic
DEAD STOCK
DVD'S

The old robots, with the love and support of the new robots, came to realize that their skills— though outdated—still held value. It was at that moment that they understood that they were not useless artifacts but rather robots to be celebrated.

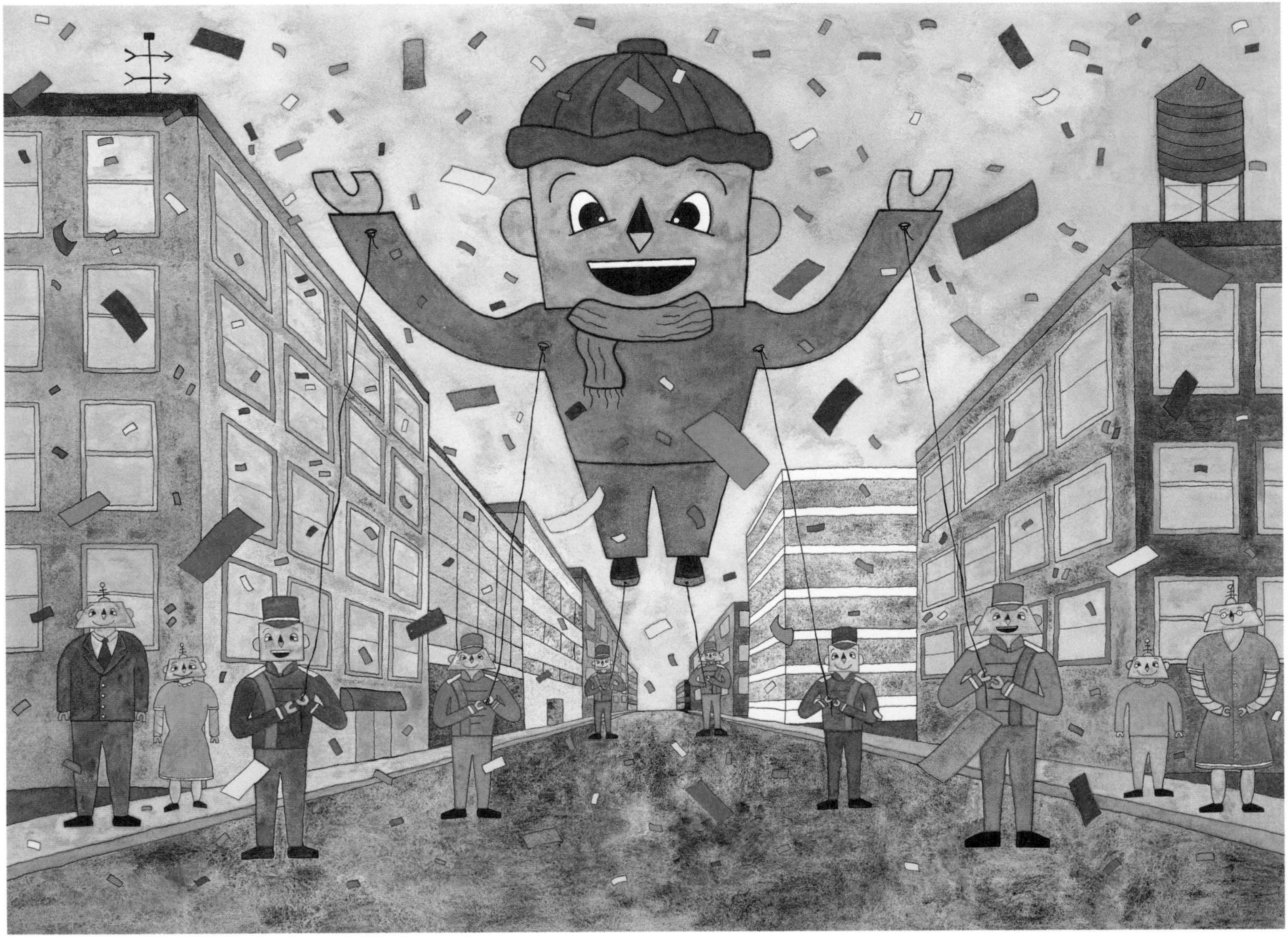

The old robots began to
content themselves with the
simple pleasures of the Bot-Life:
passing on their knowledge and
experience to an eager generation
of new robots.

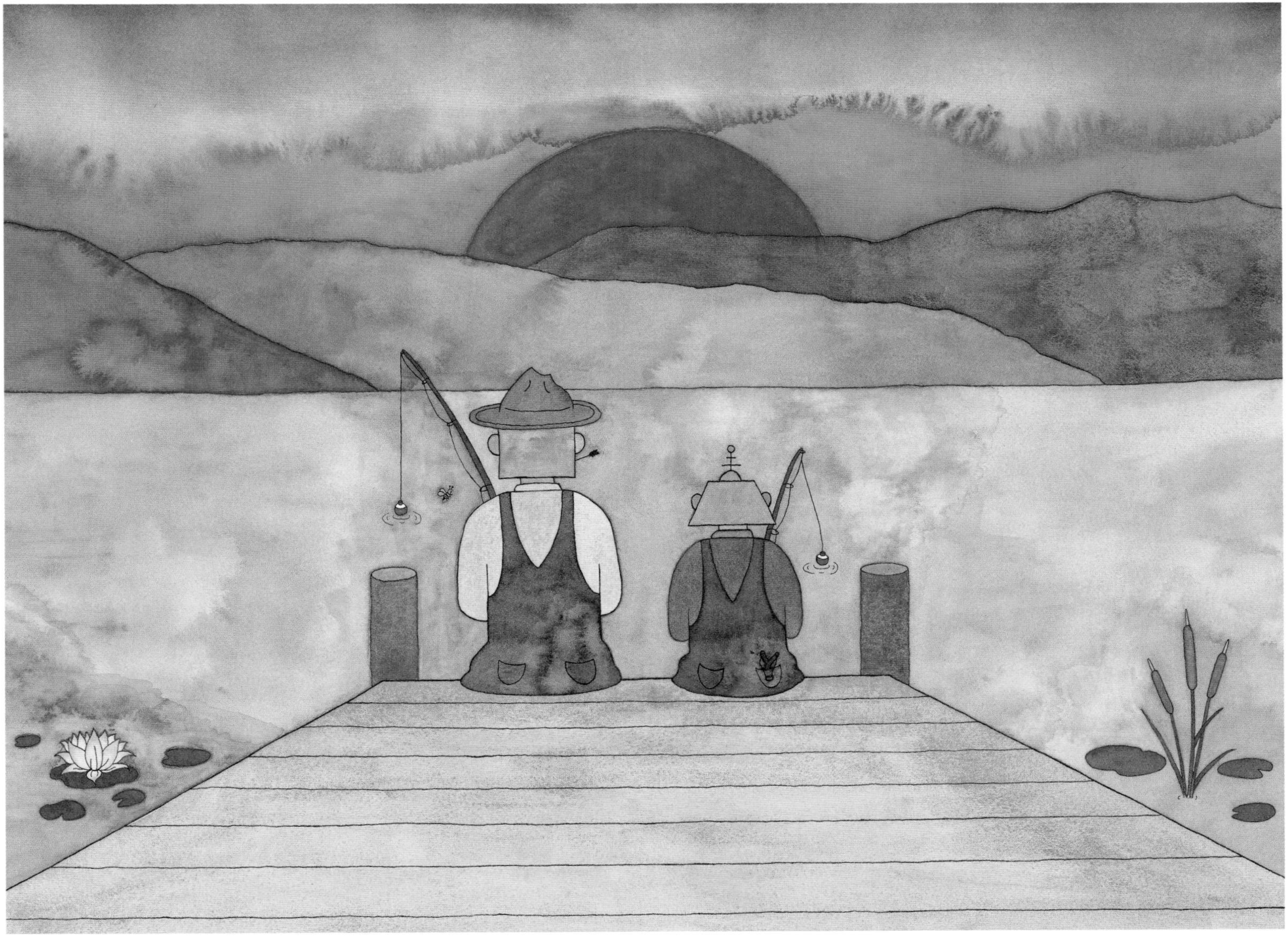

Not long afterward, the new robots created even *newer* robots that were better and faster and more efficient than themselves…

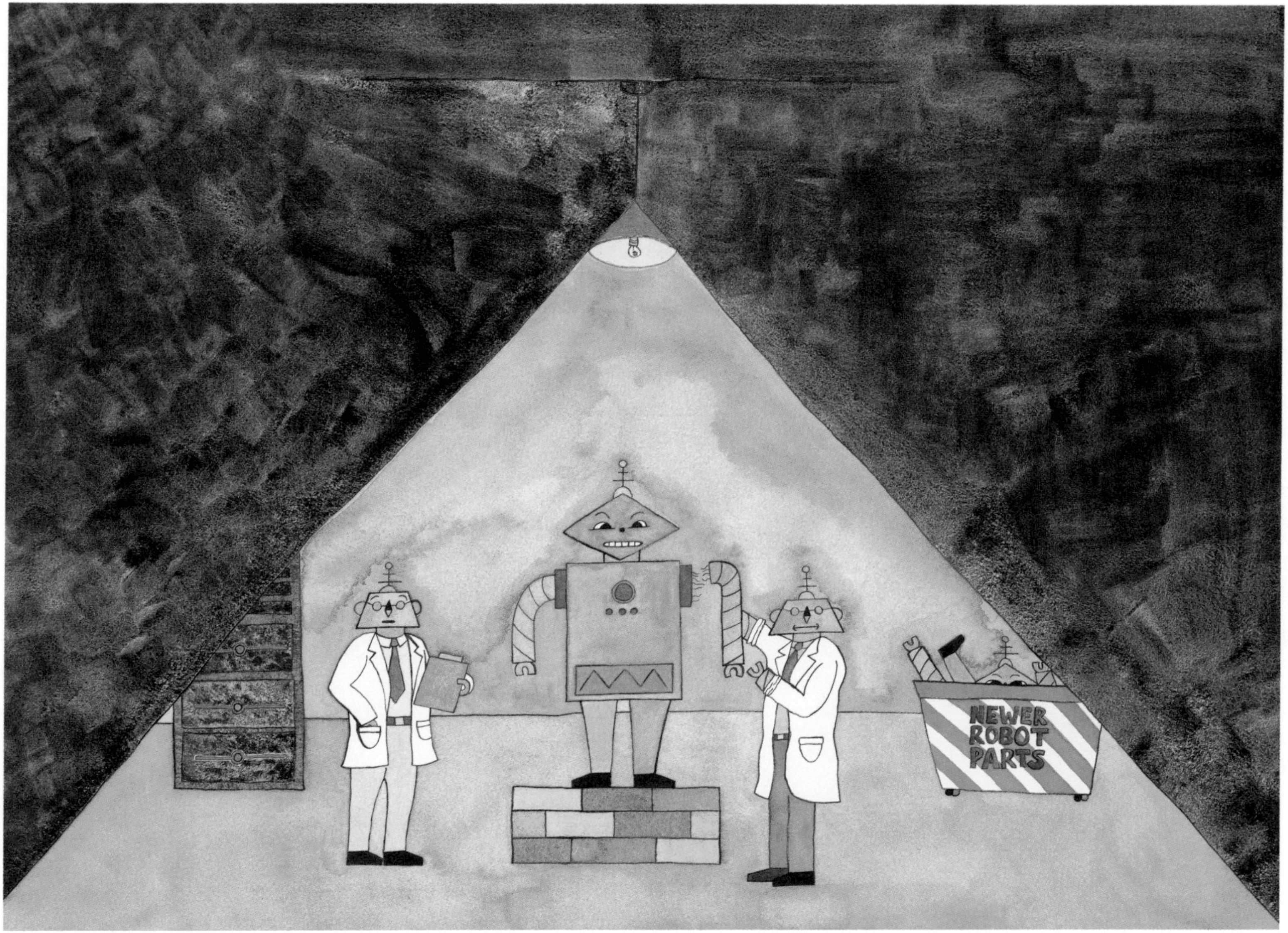
NEWER
ROBOT
PARTS

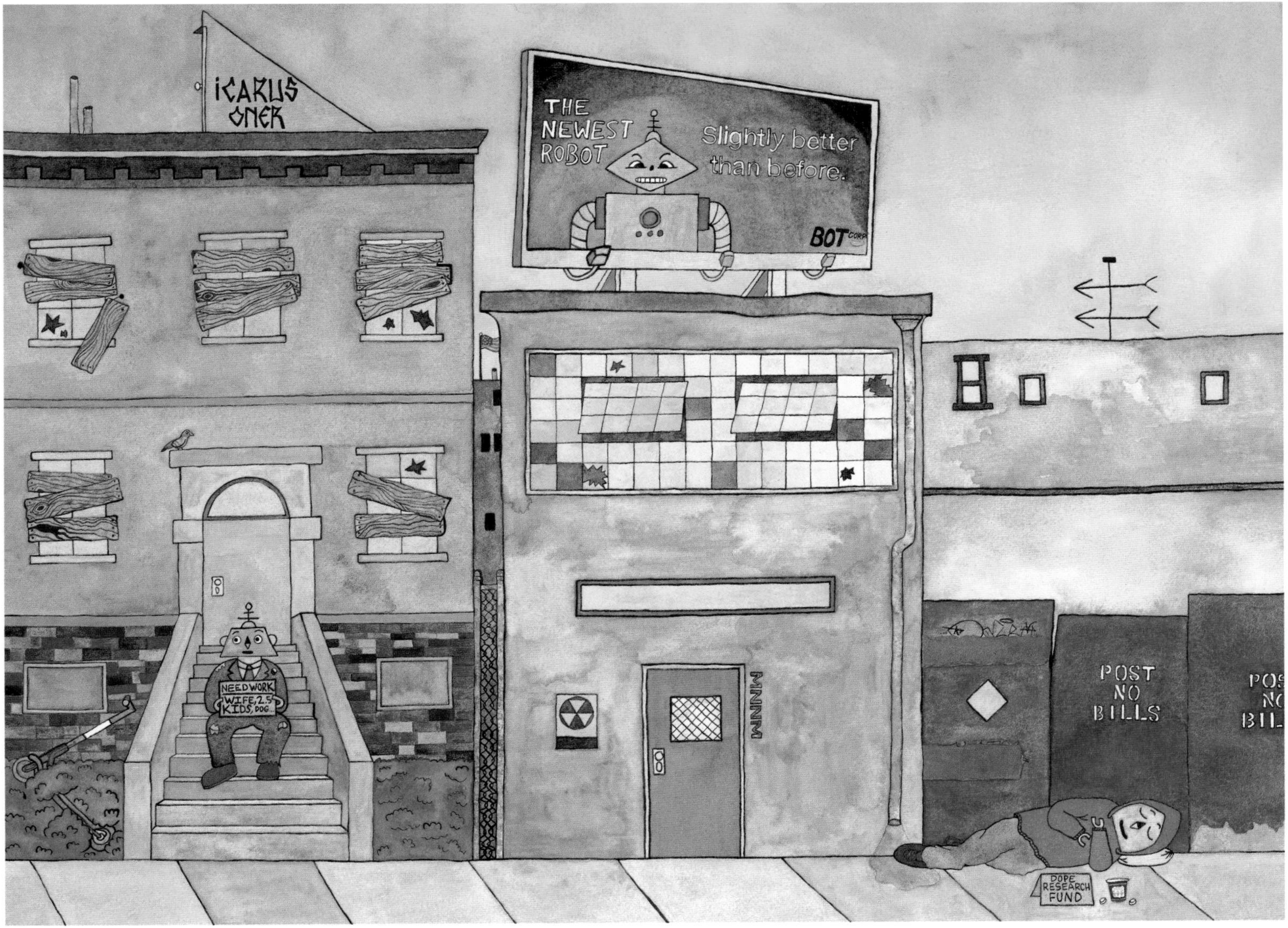

ICARUS ONER
THE NEWEST ROBOT
Slightly better than before.
BOT
NEED WORK
WIFE, 2.5 KIDS, DOG...
POST NO BILLS
DOPE RESEARCH FUND

Authors

ALEX ZOHAR is an artist, illustrator, and writer who lives and works in Los Angeles. Professionally, he's worked in the tech world for several startups and digital advertising agencies. His work has been shown in gallery exhibitions, public art projects, brand collaborations, and print publications.

Photo: Claudia Lucia

GREG FASS built a name for himself as a brand marketer and strategist for direct-to-consumer e-commerce brands. Although he still works as a brand marketer by day, he conceived of this dark comedy via a daydream about a future world where robots develop human problems to cope with progress.

Overeducated and underemployed, **JAKE RICHARDSON** started his writing career drafting contracts as a corporate lawyer but has since escaped his legal overlords and lived to tell the tale...via an illustrated graphic novella. He continues to fight the good fight against the evil BotCorp.